The Bible and the Environment

Biblical Challenges in the Contemporary World

Editor: J. W. Rogerson, University of Sheffield

Current uses of the Bible in debates about issues such as human sexuality, war and wealth and poverty often amount to either a literalist concentration on a few selected texts, or an accommodation of the Bible to secular trends. The "Biblical Challenges" series aims to acquaint readers with the biblical material pertinent to particular issues, including that which causes difficulty or embarrassment in today's world, together with suggestions about how the Bible can nonetheless present a challenge in the contemporary age. The series seeks to open up a critical dialogue between the Bible and the chosen issue, which will lead to a dialogue between the biblical text and readers, challenging them to reflection and praxis. Each volume is designed with the needs of undergraduate and college students in mind, and can serve as a course book either for a complete unit or a component.

Published:

According to the Scriptures?
The Challenge of Using the Bible in Social, Moral and Political Questions
J. W. Rogerson

The City in Biblical Perspective
J.W. Rogerson and John Vincent

Forthcoming:

Fundamentalism and the Bible
Harriet A. Harris

Science and Miracle, Faith and Doubt
A Scientific Theology of the Bible
Mark Harris

The Bible and the Environment
Towards a Critical Ecological Biblical Theology

David G. Horrell

LONDON   OAKVILLE

Published by

UK: Equinox Publishing Ltd., 1 Chelsea Manor Studios, Flood Street, London SW3 55R
USA: DBBC, 28 Main Street, Oakville, CT 06779

www.equinoxpub.com

First published 2010

British Library Cataloguing-in-Publication Data

A catalogue record for this book is available from the British Library.

ISBN   978 184553 621 3   (hardback)
            978 184553 622 0   (paperback)

Library of Congress Cataloging-in-Publication Data

Horrell, David G.
The Bible and the environment : towards a critical ecological biblical
theology / David G. Horrell.
    p. cm. -- (Biblical challenges in the contemporary world)
Includes bibliographical references (p.   ) and indexes.
ISBN 978-1-84553-621-3 (hb) — ISBN 978-1-84553-622-0 (pb) 1. Human
ecology—Biblical teaching. 2. Human ecology—Religious
aspects—Christianity. I. Title.
BS660.H67 2010
261.8'8—dc22

                        2009027167

Typeset by S.J.I. Services, New Delhi
Printed and bound in Great Britain by Lightning Source (UK) Ltd, Milton Keynes

CONTENTS

PREFACE

In the five years or so that I have worked on the material that reaches published form in this book the prominence and perceived urgency of environmental issues have steadily increased. Few would now need any convincing that such issues are among the most significant contemporary challenges calling for serious reflection and action, and few Christians would deny the importance of reconsidering what the Bible might contribute to a response to that challenge. Of course, many theologians, ethicists, and biblical scholars have already engaged with the Bible in their own attempts to develop a response to questions of ecotheology and environmental ethics. What I seek to do in this book is, first, to outline and categorize the kinds of approach to the Bible that there have been; second, to survey a range of the most obviously relevant biblical texts and consider their possible meanings and varied interpretations; and third, to offer proposals for an ecological hermeneutic. As will become clear, I argue that an approach to engaging the Bible in Christian theology must acknowledge the diversity, ambivalence, and, at times, problematic character of the biblical material, and recognize that the task of developing an ecological biblical theology requires a constructive and critical engagement with this varied material.

Those statements will indicate that my approach in this book is one located in the Christian tradition, engaging with the Christian Bible and debates about its interpretation and significance. I make this point in order to make clear the focus of the discussion and its main parameters (and to explain, for example, why I generally refer to the "Old Testament", since these Hebrew scriptures are being read primarily in their context within the Christian Bible). One other practical observation may also be useful to readers: I have provided a selected list of further reading at the end of each chapter. The first item in such lists normally offers a general introductory treatment of the relevant topic, with the remainder of the list presented in an order that broadly follows the outline of the chapter; all the items are intended to be useful for those wishing to follow up the discussion more fully. A comprehensive list of the works cited in each chapter is provided in the final bibliography.

As usual, though even more so in this case, I am greatly indebted to others who have supported and informed the writing of this book. Most of the work has been completed during a three-year project in the Centre for Biblical Studies at the University of Exeter entitled "Uses of the Bible in Environmental Ethics", funded by the Arts and Humanities Research Council of the UK (Grant No. AH D001188/1). I would like to express sincere thanks for the AHRC's support. The project has been a collaborative one, and much of the material in this book could not have been conceived and written without the ideas, research, and fruitful engagement of other members of the project team. I would like here to thank them all: Dominic Coad, Cherryl Hunt, Jonathan Morgan, Christopher Southgate, and Francesca Stavrakopoulou. In particular I would like to thank Francesca and Cherryl for their helpful comments on a draft of this book, and Cherryl and Chris for their hugely important contributions to the collaborative work we have undertaken. I cite a number of our collaborative publications in what follows, since these have fundamentally shaped and informed the material I here present, especially in Chapter 2. Readers interested to pursue more detailed, scholarly treatments of these ideas should consult these publications (see also http://www.huss.ex.ac.uk/theology/research/ubee.htm). I would also like to thank members of our advisory board (in various capacities and at various times) for very valuable support and advice: Edward Adams, John Barton, Stephen Barton, Esther Reed and John Rogerson. The project also gained a great deal from our two international visiting professors, Ernst Conradie and Harry Maier, to whom I would also like to express my sincere thanks. The influence of Conradie's work in particular will be clear in the chapters that follow, particularly towards the end of the book.

I am also very grateful to John Rogerson and the members of the Bible and Society group, for opportunities to present and discuss this work, for many helpful comments, and encouragement to contribute it to the *Biblical Challenges* series. I would also like to express my thanks to colleagues and students in the Department of Theology and Religion at the University of Exeter for providing, as ever, such a happy and stimulating context in which to work. Thanks are especially due to the students who, over a number of years, have taken courses on the Bible and environmental ethics, or on ecological hermeneutics, and have thus helped to test the material presented below and to shape my own thinking on it. Finally, I would like to thank Caroline, Emily and Cate, for making so happy the most important context of all, our home (and also to thank Caroline for reading and commenting on a draft of this book). Like many young children, Emily and Cate display that marvellous ethical "naivety" which so powerfully challenges the "realism" of adult compromise. I cannot resist recalling one small incident. After watching a TV programme about the annual Arctic ice-melt, and the threat to species there (especially polar bears) due to the impact of global warming, they initiated a change we had long hoped to make: sleeping without any lights on in the house. They hated it, but insisted nonetheless, "to help the polar bears". This is, in a sense, a very trivial example, but it illustrates nonetheless the kind of "other-regard" that might lie at the centre of a biblical ecological ethic (see pp. 140–41 below). I dedicate this book with profound love and gratitude to Emily and Cate, in the hope – a far from certain one – that the world we bequeath to them will be beautiful, diverse, and hospitable to their flourishing, and perhaps, in time, to their children's flourishing too.

David G. Horrell
Exeter, May 2009

 Arts & Humanities
Research Council

Each year the AHRC provides funding from the Government to support research and postgraduate study in the arts and humanities, from archaeology and English literature to design and dance. Only applications of the highest quality and excellence are funded and the range of research supported by this investment of public funds not only provides social and cultural benefits but also contributes to the economic success of the UK. For further information on the AHRC, please see our website www.ahrc.ac.uk

ABBREVIATIONS

BNTC	Black's New Testament Commentaries
EB	The Earth Bible
ESV	English Standard Version
KJV	King James Version
LXX	Septuagint (Old Greek)
NIV	New International Version
NRSV	New Revised Standard Version
NTG	New Testament Guides
OTG	Old Testament Guides
OTL	Old Testament Library
SBL	Society of Biblical Literature
WBC	Word Biblical Commentary
WUNT	Wissenschaftliche Untersuchungen zum Neuen Testament

Part I

READING THE BIBLE IN LIGHT OF THE ECOLOGICAL CRISIS:
APPROACHES TO INTERPRETATION

Chapter 1

THE ECOLOGICAL CRISIS AND THE CHALLENGE TO THE CHRISTIAN TRADITION

Just a few decades ago, environmental issues were somewhat at the margins of political debate. Concerns were raised about the impact of human activity on the natural world in the early 1960s, notably in Rachel Carson's classic *Silent Spring*, which highlighted the impact of chemical pesticides in particular (Carson 2000 [1962]). Carson's hugely influential book, Linda Lear notes, "initiated the contemporary environmental movement" (Lear 1999: 258). Also at the beginning of what has since become a gathering tide, Joseph Sittler, in a 1961 address to the World Council of Churches calling for ecumenical unity, noted the gravity of the threat to nature, and saw in the cosmic Christology of Colossians 1 a doctrinal basis with which to draw all of creation into the orbit of God's redemption (Sittler 2000b [1962]; see ch. 7 below). Indeed, already in the 1950s Sittler was articulating the need for a "theology for earth", a theology which would rekindle a positive view of the earth as bound up in God's redemptive work (Sittler 2000a [1954]). In 1967, Lynn White Jr, to whose classic article we shall shortly return, spoke of "our ecologic crisis", holding Western Christianity largely to blame. "Green" activists and pressure groups emerged – with Greenpeace and Friends of the Earth both formed in 1971 – which campaigned on issues from nuclear power and industrial pollution to pesticides and waste disposal. But "green" issues mostly remained somewhat at the margins of political and public debate.

During the 1980s there was a widespread growth in awareness of environmental concerns, with landmark moments such as the discovery in 1985 of the ozone depletion over Antarctica – a discovery which quite rapidly led to a series of international agreements concerning the use of CFCs, these being responsible for this ozone impact (see Maslin 2007 [2002]: 21–22). In the subsequent years there has been a gradually increasing focus on environmental issues in general, and global warming in particular.

In the last few years, the degree of focus has rapidly intensified. The subject of global warming has gained enormous attention, and is now recognized by governments the world over as one of the key issues demanding international action now and in the coming years. As Michael Northcott already noted in 1996, "[t]he single most pervasive and potentially cataclysmic factor in the ecological crisis is that of climate change" (Northcott 1996: 2). Quite rapidly, the debate has shifted from the question of *whether* human activity is causing global warming, to a question predicated on the scientific consensus that this is indeed the case: How can we act to avert, or at least to mitigate, what seem to be the potentially enormous consequences of the climatic changes already being caused by global warming? It is becoming increasingly clear that massive and immediate reductions in CO_2 emissions are required in order to ameliorate the likely impact of ongoing global warming, but there are questions about whether the political will exists to deal decisively and swiftly with the situation. The state of the evidence is briefly summarized by Mark Maslin:

> The most recent [2001] report by the Intergovernmental Panel on Climate Change (IPCC), shows there is clear evidence for a 1.1°F (0.6°C) rise in global temperatures and a 7¾ in (20 cm) rise in sea level during the twentieth century. There is evidence for a 40 per cent reduction in the thickness of sea ice over the Arctic Ocean. Mountain glaciers are melting at the fastest rate ever recorded. There has been a 40 per cent increase in storm activity in the North Atlantic region over the last 50 years and global floods and droughts have become more frequent. In England, the winter of 2000/2001 was the wettest on record, while the heat wave in 2003 killed at least 35,000 people in Europe. The IPCC report predicts that global temperatures will rise by up to 10.4°F (5.8°C) by 2100. (Maslin 2007: 7)

The precise impact of global warming in the near and distant future is harder to predict, given the difficulties entailed in modelling the processes involved. But the likely scenarios include the following (see Maslin 2007: 39–55). (1) Increased sea-levels and associated flooding will have a massive impact on countries with large populations living in low-lying areas, such as Bangladesh and Thailand, and will make some islands, such as the Maldives, uninhabitable. (2) More frequent and violent storms and floods will mean that "the Caribbean, United States, and Central America ... will be hit more often and by bigger, more violent, hurricanes" (Maslin 2007: 48). (3) Rapid climate change will lead to the depletion or extinction of plant and animal species; coral reefs are one example of an ecosystem under particular threat. (4) Agriculture will be affected by changes in climate, and some areas may become uncultivatable. Crops which are particularly sensitive to variations in temperature and moisture supply are especially vulnerable. (5) Water supplies will also be affected, such that relatively wet countries will become wetter, while those prone to drought will become still drier. (6) Finally, some diseases may become more prevalent and dangerous given the increased warmth and moisture associated with global warming. Malaria, for example, may well spread "due to expansion of the areas suitable for malaria transmission ... The incidence of infection is most sensitive to climate changes in areas of Southeast Asia, South America and parts of Africa. Global warming will also provide for the first time ever the right conditions for mosquitoes to breed in Southern England, Europe and the northern United States" (Maslin 2007: 54). The latest (2007) report of the IPCC affirms and intensifies the scale of the threat, consolidating the scientific evidence for human-induced global warming and clarifying the scale of the likely changes (see IPCC 2007).

While global warming is the most prominent environmental issue attracting political and public concern, there are plenty of other topics too, with impacts ranging from the local to the global: waste disposal, pollution, the reduction of biodiversity through species loss, the destruction of ecosystems, the loss of fertile topsoils and accessible water supplies. The list of issues could go on (see Northcott 1996: 1–32; Bouma-Prediger 2001: 39–66 for discussion of key issues and statistics). Again, the statistics paint a sobering picture: it has been estimated that "around 10,000 species are destroyed annually as a consequence of human activity in the natural world" (Northcott 1996: 21). "Tropical forests are currently destroyed at the rate of twenty-five million acres per year", an area equivalent in size to the state of Indiana (Bouma-Prediger 2001: 47). And quite apart from the intrinsic worth we might ascribe to all such species and ecosystems, the impact of human activity adds to the immense suffering of millions of the world's poorest people, who experience the worst impacts of polluted water supplies, loss of fertile lands, and the increased risk of flooding consequent upon global warming (see Clifford 2007).

In a recent study, James Martin-Schramm and Robert Stivers offer a concise diagnosis of the major causes of such problems:

> Environmental degradation is a product of five interrelated causes: (1) too many people, (2) some of whom are consuming too much, (3) using powerful technologies that frequently damage nature's ecosystems, (4) supported by economic and political systems that permit and even encourage degradation, and (5) informed by anthropocentric attitudes toward nature. (Martin-Schramm and Stivers 2003: 10)

World population, they note, is now at around 6 billion and increasing by roughly 1.3% p.a. (p. 10). The UN has predicted that it will grow to 9 billion by 2050 before beginning to stabilize (p. 11). Whatever the precise figures in the future, the sheer numbers of human beings now on the planet already place enormous demands upon its natural resources, and this will only increase.

But this pressure is particularly exerted by people in the richer countries of the world, given their levels of material consumption. "The quantities", Martin-Schramm and Stivers note, "are staggering by any historical measure" (p. 11). Technological developments – which can of course bring positive benefits as well as negative impacts – enable industrial and commercial activities on a huge scale and with correspondingly huge impacts; one need only think of the impact of the development of the internal combustion engine. To compound the problem, they note that "high levels of consumption are critical to the functioning of modern capitalism" (p. 12); economic growth and ever-expanding consumption are essential to the system. Moreover, with many countries in the world, China and India perhaps the most prominent examples, seeking to develop and expand economically at as fast a rate as possible – not least in order to alleviate the poverty of their citizens – the pressures of production and consumption seem only likely to increase. And developing countries understandably object when the richest countries of the world, who have already reaped the benefit of exploiting not only their own natural resources but those of other countries too, now try to restrain the activity of those who would like a share in the prosperity.

Yet it is the last factor that Martin-Schramm and Stivers mention that is of particular interest to us: "anthropocentric [i.e., human-centred] attitudes toward nature". This points to an aspect of the causes of our environmental problems that lies not so much in production or consumption, in agriculture or industry *per se*, but rather in the kind of attitudes, or worldview, that people have. Religion in general, and the biblical tradition specifically, is arguably of key significance in shaping people's worldview, their understanding of the way things are, their place in the world, and their relationship to that which is around them.

Indeed, this is precisely the argument of Lynn White Jr in a 1967 article that has become the most cited piece in the whole ecotheological debate. White argued that it is the Christian worldview, as it developed in Western Christianity, that legitimated and encouraged humanity's aggressive project to dominate and exploit nature. The basic reason for this is that "[e]specially in its Western form, Christianity is the most anthropocentric religion the world has seen" (White 1967: 1205). According to this worldview, White suggests, everything that exists in the natural world was "planned" by God "explicitly for man's benefit and rule; no item in the physical creation had any purpose save to serve man's purposes". Humanity is seen as uniquely made in the image of God, and as given "dominion" over all the creatures of the earth (Gen 1.26–30). Sweeping aside other ancient mythologies, with their cyclical views of time and their animistic sacralization of nature, Christianity thus "not only established a dualism of man and nature but also insisted that it is God's will that man exploit nature for his proper ends … Man's effective monopoly … was confirmed and the old inhibitions to the exploitation of nature crumbled." Thus, "Christianity made it possible to exploit nature in a mood of indifference to the feelings of natural objects" (p. 1205). White concludes that the active conquest of nature that characterizes the modern technological project and has led to the "ecologic crisis" has in large part been made possible by the dominance in the West of this Christian world-view. Christianity therefore "bears a huge burden of guilt" (p. 1206).

However, White does not dismiss the Christian tradition out of hand; he appeals to the figure of St Francis as a positive model, a potential "patron saint for ecologists" (p. 1207). Also important is White's insistence that religious worldviews are of profound importance in shaping our actions; he does not see salvation in secularism:

> What people do about their ecology depends on what they think about themselves in relation to things around them. Human ecology is deeply conditioned by beliefs about our nature and destiny – that is, by religion … More science and more technology are not going to get us out of the present ecologic crisis until we find a new religion, or rethink our old one. (White 1967: 1205–06)

According to White, then, Christianity, and the creation stories on which its views of humanity and the world are based, bear a large responsibility for introducing the kind of worldview that has legitimated and encouraged aggressive human domination and exploitation of nature, and thus brought about our present "ecologic crisis".

Also crucial to consider is the influence of biblical eschatology; that is, the view of the "end-times" (Greek *eschata* means "last things") presented in various biblical books. A number of biblical texts appear to present images of cosmic destruction in their depictions of what will happen on "the day of the Lord", a biblical label for the coming day of God's judgement and salvation (see, e.g., Joel 1.15; Amos 5.18–20; 1 Thess. 5.2). Some texts suggest that catastrophes on the earth must precede this final day of salvation (e.g., Mark 13); others depict Christians being "caught up" to meet the returning Lord in the air (1 Thess. 4.16–17). Such texts, along with the enigmatic apocalyptic scenarios depicted in the book of Revelation, have, of course, shaped the development of contemporary Christian eschatologies. For example, some evangelical Christians anticipate a "rapture" of Christians from the earth, prior to a time of great tribulation; some believe that the return of Christ will happen suddenly, and may well be imminent (see ch. 2 below). The critical question is whether such eschatological views, explicitly or implicitly, foster a view of the earth as merely a temporary and soon-to-be destroyed home for humans, from which the elect will be rescued. The implication would be that preserving the earth is hardly a priority, and may even represent opposition to the progress of God's eschatological purposes. Indeed, some writers have argued that such views make evangelical Christians disinclined to care for the earth. David Orr, for example, suggests that "belief in the imminence of the end times tends to make evangelicals careless stewards of our forests, soils, wildlife, air, water, seas and climate" (Orr 2005: 291). Just as White's seminal article raised critical questions about the impact of the biblical creation stories, so the arguments of Orr and others raise critical questions about the impact of biblical eschatology on Christian attitudes towards the environment.

Many theologians and biblical scholars have responded to such criticisms, often attempting to defend Christianity and the Bible against these kinds of accusations. One central question is indeed of fundamental importance: Does the Christian tradition really inculcate an ecologically damaging worldview? White's essay in particular, although it does not explicitly engage with biblical texts, raises the question as to whether this Christian worldview, with its positioning of humankind as supreme over creation, is one constructed and promoted by the Bible itself. Similarly, we may ask how far a world-negating, anti-environmental stance is encouraged by the Bible's eschatological visions. Such questions begin to indicate the agenda for this book. Our task is to consider what kind of views of the earth and the rich diversity of life upon it are presented in the Bible. How is humanity depicted in relation to non-human life? How are relationships between God, humanity, and the earth understood? How are the Bible's visions of the future to be understood and interpreted? Can the Bible be defended against criticisms of the kind raised by White, or does it indeed promote a worldview which is anthropocentric – human-centred – in such a way as to underpin and sustain our aggressive and self-serving exploitation of the non-human world?

Addressing such questions will, of course, involve us looking at a range of the most relevant biblical texts, trying to ascertain their possible meaning(s) and the kind of view of relationships between humanity, God, and the earth that they present. But it will also involve us looking at the kinds of approaches to interpretation of the Bible that are practised by various contributors to this debate. As we shall see, the question of *hermeneutics* – that is, our approach to interpretation – is crucial to any consideration of the ecological implications of biblical texts. Indeed, to anticipate my overall argument, I will suggest, and attempt to demonstrate in what follows, that what we need is not merely a careful reading of biblical texts, but to articulate and develop an ecological hermeneutic, that is, a newly reorientated way of reading the Bible that is demanded by our current context and the issues that face us.

In order to explore and develop this argument through the book, we need first to explore the different kinds of approach to the Bible that have been taken by those either promoting or opposing an ethics of responsible care for the environment. Illustrating the different kinds of reading strategy, and the different assumptions and commitments that underpin them, will help to alert us to the various ways in which the texts might be approached when in the chapters that follow I survey a range of biblical texts of apparent relevance to environmental issues. Inevitably, due to both the limitations of space and the need to survey critically current discussion, the focus falls mostly on those texts already identified as crucial and relevant to environmental questions. The following chapters will illustrate, albeit selectively, something of the range of perspectives evident in the Bible. But, equally importantly, they will illustrate the various readings to which the texts are open, and which scholars debate. Finally, in the closing section of the book, as I draw the overall argument to a conclusion, I attempt the task outlined above: to sketch the elements of an ecological hermeneutic. What exactly this means, and what its substantive content might be, it is the task of this book to set out.

Further reading

Maslin, Mark, *Global Warming* (Revised edn, WorldLife Library; Grantown-on-Spey, Scotland: Colin Baxter Photography, 2007).
——, *Global Warming: A Very Short Introduction* (Oxford: OUP, 2004).
IPCC, *Climate Change 2007: Synthesis Report,* at http://www.ipcc.ch/publications_and_data/publications_ipcc_fourth_assessment_report_synthesis_report.htm

Bouma-Prediger, Steven, *For the Beauty of the Earth: A Christian Vision for Creation Care* (Grand Rapids, MI: Baker Academic, 2001), 39–66.

Martin-Schramm, James B. and Stivers, Robert L., *Christian Environmental Ethics: A Case Study Approach* (Maryknoll, NY: Orbis, 2003), 9–32.

Northcott, Michael S., *The Environment and Christian Ethics* (New Studies in Christian Ethics; Cambridge: Cambridge University Press, 1996), 1–39.

White, Lynn, Jr, "The Historical Roots of our Ecologic Crisis", *Science* 155 (1967) 1203–07.

Orr, David W., "Armageddon Versus Extinction", *Conservation Biology* 19 (2005) 290–92.

Chapter 2

Approaches to Reading the Bible in Relation to Environmental Issues

Recovering ecological wisdom from the Bible

As we noted in the opening chapter, Lynn White's challenge to Christianity has served as a provocative stimulus to much theological and biblical study. As Ernst Conradie notes, many biblical contributions to ecological theology have been "deliberately aimed at defending Christianity against the accusations of Lynn White" (Conradie 2004: 126). In other words, in a good deal of such biblical and theological reflection there has been an attempt to show that the biblical tradition – contrary to the criticism of White – offers positive and valuable resources for a stance of environmental action and concern. Since such approaches to the Bible represent a defensive stance, they may, following Paul Santmire, be labelled "apologetic": their aim is to show, despite criticism, that the Bible does offer positive resources to support Christian environmental care (Santmire 2000: 7). Alternatively, this approach may be labelled a strategy of *recovery*, that is, one which seeks the recovery or retrieval of the Bible's ecological wisdom, a wisdom that has been hidden and obscured by interpreters who failed to see or attend to such dimensions of the text (see Horrell *et al.* 2008: 221–25).

One may usefully compare this approach with that taken by some writers dealing with the topic of women in the Bible: their claim, likewise, has been that it is possible to retrieve a positive picture of male-female equality, of the participation of women in leadership, and so on, from a careful reading of the texts, despite the tendency of (male) interpreters to deny or miss this. The description of Eve as Adam's "helper" (*'ezer*), for example, in Gen. 2:18–25, should not, it is argued, be taken to indicate the woman's lowly or subordinate status but rather her importance and influence (Trible 1993: 42). Or in Rom. 16:7, where interpreters and translations have tended to assume that the name *Iounian* must refer to a man named Junias, since he (!) is named as "prominent among the apostles", it is now widely accepted that it is much more likely to refer to a woman named Junia, who may even be regarded as the first woman apostle (Epp 2005). More broadly, Jesus and Paul may be depicted as some kind of early feminists, liberating women from cultural constraints and welcoming them as equals (Klassen 1984).

In relation to environmental issues, and recalling the critique mounted by White, such readings of recovery attempt to rescue biblical texts from the accusation that they promote an anthropocentric worldview which legitimizes aggressive domination of the earth. Genesis 1:26–28, where humanity is apparently given a mandate to subdue the earth, is one text which has (for obvious reasons) been subject to such defence. A number of authors, as we shall see in Chapter 3, have maintained that this text does not have in view any kind of aggressive technological domination of the earth. Positively, it is often argued that the kind of role the Bible does prescribe for humanity in relation to creation is one of "stewardship" – a responsible, caring, and sustaining role, not one of exploitation or thoughtless mismanagement. Thus the Bible is seen as the source of a positive ecological theology – a claim embodied in the recently published *Green Bible* (HarperCollins, 2008).

It is notable that certain key texts have become the established favourites for such positive ecological engagement with the Bible. These are texts which, it may be argued, most clearly provide the basis for a positive attitude to the earth and thus help to undergird an ethic of environmental responsibility. These favourite texts include Genesis 1–2, Gen. 9:1–17; Psalm 104; Rom. 8:18–25; Col. 1:15–20; and Revelation 21–22. Others of course are also discussed. Steven Bouma-Prediger, for example, sets out a biblical "story" to underpin an ecological theology by drawing on Genesis 1, Genesis 9, Job 38–41, Col. 1:15–20 and Revelation 21–22 (Bouma-Prediger 2001: 87–116). As well as texts which appear to offer a positive contribution, certain texts are also a focus of attention because of the particular difficulties they raise. We have already seen that Gen. 1:26–28 is one such text; others include texts that depict an apparent end for the earth, especially 2 Pet. 3:10–13. Those who attempt a reading of recovery need to show that these texts are not as damaging for an ecological theology as they are sometimes thought to be (cf. Bouma-Prediger 2001: 73–80). While a prominent defensive strategy in relation to Gen. 1:26–28 has been to interpret it as reflective of the idea of stewardship, the most common strategy with regard to the eschatological texts such as 2 Pet. 3:10–13 has been to argue that these texts envisage not destruction but transformation of the earth (see further ch. 9; Finger 1998).

Suspicion and resistance

These kinds of readings of "recovery", then, examples of which we shall see in the following chapters, represent attempts to show that the Bible can and does offer the resources for a positive view of the environment and for an ethic of care for creation. A different kind of approach is taken by authors who consider that the Bible does, at least in places, inculcate a damaging form of anthropocentrism which relegates the earth to a secondary status and value. In a sense, such authors agree with White, at least in part, in finding some parts of the Bible responsible for generating attitudes that lead humans to regard themselves as superior rulers of the world, with the world's resources available to be exploited for human benefit. Committed to ecological values, these authors argue that such biblical texts must be exposed and resisted. In contrast to a stance of "recovery", we may label such an approach to the Bible a strategy of *resistance* (see Horrell *et al.* 2008: 225–28). Again, a parallel may be drawn with some feminist writings, where the biblical texts are regarded and exposed as irredeemably patriarchal and sexist, promoting values that are deeply damaging to women. For some writers, such as Mary Daly and Daphne Hampson, the Christian tradition as a whole is so thoroughly patriarchal that it must be rejected and replaced. Similarly, some ecological thinkers have suggested that the Christian tradition cannot provide the kind of valuing of the earth that our contemporary context demands, and so again must be rejected. More often, however, it is *certain* biblical texts that are shown to be problematic due to their depiction of women in relation to men, or of earth in relation to humanity. In other words, this kind of approach insists that the Bible needs to be read with both suspicion and sympathy; it requires the exercise of both resistance and recovery, depending, in part, on the particular text in view.

Some examples of this kind of approach may be found in the five-volume Earth Bible series, the main output to date of the ongoing Earth Bible Project, based in Adelaide, Australia. These volumes, produced by members of the Earth Bible Team, offer the most extensive attempt to engage in an ecologically-orientated reading of biblical texts "from the perspective of Earth" (see Habel 2000c; 2001b; Habel and Wurst 2000; 2001; Habel and Balabanski 2002). Fundamental to the studies produced by the Team is a set of six ecojustice principles:

1. *The principle of intrinsic worth*: The universe, Earth and all its components have intrinsic worth/value;

2. *The principle of interconnectedness*: Earth is a community of interconnected living things that are mutually dependent on each other for life and survival;

3. *The principle of voice*: Earth is a subject capable of raising its voice in celebration and against injustice;

4. *The principle of purpose*: The universe, Earth and all its components, are part of a dynamic cosmic design within which each piece has a place in the overall goal of that design.

5. *The principle of mutual custodianship*: Earth is a balanced and diverse domain where responsible custodians can function as partners, rather than rulers, to sustain a balanced and diverse Earth community.

6. *The principle of resistance*: Earth and its components not only suffer from injustices at the hands of humans, but actively resist them in the struggle for justice. (Habel 2000c: 24)

These principles set out the stance from which the biblical texts are read, a set of ethical convictions which reflect a commitment to what the Team call "ecojustice". These principles effectively form a kind of ethical standard against which the biblical texts are measured: the key task is to discern whether "the text is consistent, or in conflict, with whichever of the six ecojustice principles may be considered relevant" in any particular case (Earth Bible Team 2002: 2). Where the texts cohere with the principles, they may be fruitfully and positively read; where they do not, suspicion and resistance may be more appropriate interpretative strategies. The volumes of the Earth Bible series therefore contain examples of readings of recovery and of resistance, depending on the texts in view – and, of course, on the stance and perspective of the reader.

The studies produced by the Earth Bible Team, many of which we shall engage with through the course of this book, represent a clear and explicit commitment to ecojustice principles. Often this leads to a positive recovery of ecological wisdom in the biblical texts, a mode of interpretation we considered in the previous section. But when the texts are deemed to contradict the ecojustice principles, their anti-Earth perspectives are exposed and resisted.

There is, however, a different kind of "resistance" also evident in certain engagements between the Bible and the environmental agenda. This type of resistance is hardly represented, at least explicitly, in academic scholarship, but may nonetheless be of considerable popular influence. This kind of resistance is exactly the opposite to that found in the work of the Earth Bible Team. Rather than resist the biblical texts where they fail to measure up to ecojustice principles, in this case we are concerned with an approach which, because of its commitment to the authority of the Bible, resists the environmental agenda, either explicitly or implicitly (see Horrell *et al.* 2008: 228–31). Again, we may draw a parallel with some Christian reactions to feminism and the women's movement: rather than find support for women's equality and opportunity in the Bible, some feel that a commitment to the authority of the Bible requires an opposition to the "cultural" pressures supporting gender equality. The Bible, some insist, does teach that man is rightly head of woman, and that men rightly hold the key position of leadership and authority in both home and church. In a similar way, some have argued that loyalty to the Bible should lead Christians to reject the pressures to endorse environmentalism.

For example, books published in the 1980s by Constance Cumbey and Dave Hunt warned Christians against the dangers of the New Age movement, and saw any moves towards environmental stewardship or ecological awareness as aspects of this New Age influence, which was itself seen as a mask for a developing form of satanic tyranny (Cumbey 1983; D. Hunt 1983). More recently, Calvin Beisner (1997) has offered a forceful critique of evangelical environmentalism from an evangelical perspective. Beisner does not deny the importance of caring for the creation, and agrees that humanity has a responsibility to exercise stewardship. But he disputes much of the evidence used to suggest that there is an environmental crisis, including that concerning the impact of global warming (pp. 65–66, 164, 170). The environment, he insists, "is improving, not deteriorating" (p. 110). Beisner argues that humanity's God-given task is to turn the earth from wilderness into garden, increasing its bounty and productivity, thus reversing the effects of fall and curse (cf. chs 3–4 below). He favours unfettered economic development as the best means by which developing (as well as developed) countries can increase their wealth and improve their environments. And he does not see any need for those in the richest countries like the USA to reduce their levels of consumption. Moreover, contrary to those environmentalists who see the size of the human population as a threat, "Biblical Christians", Beisner argues, can be confident that

> continued population growth will result not in the depletion but in the increased abundance of resources, and not in increased pollution of the earth but in its increased cleansing and transformation from wilderness to garden, "from its bondage to decay … into the glorious freedom of the children of God" (Rom. 8:21). (Beisner 1997: 107; cf. p. 125, etc.)

So population growth can continue, and is, from the Christian perspective, a good thing (cf. Gen. 1:28); human ingenuity will continue to find ways to increase resource availability and productivity.

Interpretations of biblical eschatology are especially important in evangelical opposition to environmentalism (see Maier forthcoming). For example, there is the approach to interpreting biblical eschatology known as premillennial dispensationalism (see further Finger 1998: 17–24). On this view, history is divided into various phases, or divine dispensations, and will culminate in a great tribulation, a battle between good and evil (Armageddon), and a millennial reign of Christ on the earth. Prior to the tribulation, however, Christians will be raptured from the earth. While this eschatology is probably not of major influence in British and continental European Christianity, its influence in the USA is greater (see Gribben 2004: 77–79). It has a significant if indirect impact on the environmental agenda to the extent that it fosters a view of natural disasters and signs of earthly decay as indicators of the imminent end which are therefore to be welcomed. It also focuses Christian hope on the rescuing of the elect from a doomed earth, rather than (say) on the liberation and renewal of all creation (cf. Boyer 1992: 331–37; Osborn 1993: 61–63). Working to preserve the natural environment is not only pointless, it is working against God's purposes (and thus for Satan's), since the destruction of the physical elements of the cosmos must happen before the End.

This kind of reading of biblical prophecy and eschatology is evident in books such as Hal Lindsey's *The Late, Great Planet Earth* and more recently in the *Left Behind* series of novels by Tim LaHaye and Jerry Jenkins. These have sold in huge numbers and have thus exerted massive popular influence, especially in the USA (see Maier 2002; Gribben 2004: 78). It is difficult to assess the extent to which such books, and the eschatology they present, directly influence environmental attitudes and policies, but there is at least some anecdotal evidence to suggest that they might. James Watt, Ronald Reagan's Secretary of the Interior, famously testified in 1981 to the House Interior Committee concerning the difficulty of knowing how far we needed to conserve resources for future generations: "I do not know", Watt said, "how many future generations we can count on before the Lord returns" (see Boyer 1992: 141). However, despite Watt's statement being frequently quoted to suggest that he did not see preservation of resources as an issue, his statement continues, "whatever it is we have to manage with a skill to leave the resources needed for future generations" (see http://powerlineblog.com/archives/2005/02/009377.php [accessed 15 May 2009]). Nonetheless, at the very least, the idea of the Lord's (possibly imminent) return is here linked with consideration about stewardship of natural resources. Interestingly, a 1999 survey "found that 66% of Americans believe that Jesus will return in their lifetime" (Maier forthcoming). We may plausibly consider that a combination of theological tendencies and convictions – the idea of Christ's imminent return, or of a "rapture" of Christians from the earth, a focus on the conversion and salvation of (human) individuals, and so on – can easily lead to a view in which the rest of creation is, at best, of secondary importance, or at worst, a mere stage for the outworking of the drama of human salvation, destined to be destroyed as the End Times approach. Indeed, some sociological studies have indicated such a link between beliefs and environmental attitudes (though there are complex interconnections between religious and political convictions, both of which influence environmental views; see, e.g., Eckberg and Blocker 1996; Sherkat and Ellison 2007). In the words of one recent internet commentator, Christians who turn from the priorities of evangelism to environmental care are acting like a surgeon who abandons an operation to go and unblock a toilet (Strandberg [no date]).

Popular Christian opposition to the environmental movement is often based on appeals to biblical texts such as 2 Pet. 3:10–13, which are taken to teach that the "real" threat is not from so-called global warming, but rather from the fire of judgement which God will bring upon the earth (try typing "2 Peter 3" and "global warming" into an internet search engine). For example:

> Christians should not be carried away into the frenzy that is being stirred up in popular culture. While it is true that we are all stewards of the earth and should thus take care of it, we should also be aware of the fact that the "heavens and earth which are now" are being prevented from being destroyed by the Word of God (2 Pet. 3:7). God will one day destroy the earth with the fire of judgment, and this is the warning that Christians must take to those who are lost, in order that they might be saved through the obedience of the Gospel. (Strickland 2008)

Or again, in still more strident style, and specifically in opposition to Al Gore, former US vice-president, who has energetically promoted the need for decisive action to combat global warming, especially through his film *An Inconvenient Truth* (2006):

> Don't believe these politically correct biblically ignorant false prophets. The Bible warns of false teachers in the last days in II Peter 2:1–3. Making merchandise of you will be their greatest ulterior motive. That is exactly what the eco-huckster Gore is in the process of doing.

> Global warming is coming, but not the Al Gore type. II Peter 3:10–13
> states ... We should be preparing for God's global warming program, the day
> of judgment, not Al Gore's unscientific diatribe of distortions and lies.
> (Grove 2008)

With such popular views in mind, Keith Dyer has suggested (somewhat tongue in cheek) "a fundamentalist Christian version of the Earth Bible's six ecojustice principles". He calls them "the six Biblicist Eschatological principles":

1. *The principle of imminent cataclysm* – Earth is headed for disaster (sooner rather than later).
2. *The principle of disconnectedness* – we humans don't have to share or feel responsible for Earth's fate (salvation is for humans, not Earth)
3. *The principle of inevitability* – there's nothing we (or Earth) can do about it.
4. *The principle of transcendence* – what really matters is the next world ...
5. *The principle of sovereignty* – God is in ultimate (even direct) control of all this.
6. *The principle of self-interest* – God will rapture "believers" out of this mess in the nick of time. (Dyer 2002: 45)

Dyer's "principles" are, of course, a provocative and critical set, summarizing a viewpoint with which Dyer fundamentally disagrees. But they do serve well to sharpen the questions about biblical eschatologies and their contemporary interpretation: To what extent does the Bible support this kind of human-centred picture of an (imminent) End in which the earth will be destroyed and the elect rescued? And what kind of interpretation of such texts is possible, and desirable? This is an issue which is addressed in some of the following chapters (see especially chs 8–9, 11).

Conclusion

These various approaches to the reading and interpretation of the Bible differ in various ways, politically and ethically, as well as theologically. A stance of *recovery*, consistently pursued, reflects a strong commitment both to environmental values and to the authority and status of the Bible; one might even say that a commitment to both *requires* a reading which shows that the Bible is ecofriendly. If one is committed to the supreme authority of the entire Bible, as the infallible Word of God – as are many evangelical Christians, for example – and also committed to the environmental cause, then one has to find ways to show that the Bible supports that environmental commitment. Otherwise it cannot stand alongside the commitment to biblical authority. Indeed, the resistance towards the environmental agenda that emerges, explicitly or implicitly, from certain kinds of fundamentalist readings of the Bible shows how a primary commitment to the authority of the Bible – understood, of course, in a very particular way – can lead to a consequent suspicion or even rejection of environmentalism. On the other hand, the kind of resistance practised as one facet of the Earth Bible Team's ecojustice approach reflects a strong – even primary – commitment to ecojustice, and a willingness to criticize, resist and reject biblical texts where they are considered to promote a negative view of earth's status and relationship to humanity.

This brief survey of some of the ways in which the Bible has been read in relation to ecological issues illustrates how diverse have been the reading strategies employed. While some have sought to show that the Bible does have a positive "green" message to impart, if only we will listen carefully, others maintain that a proper Christian commitment to the Bible should entail a resistance to the environmental movement, which is not seen as an embodiment of Christian values. Still others have insisted that the Bible cannot naively be taken as an environmentally friendly book, but contains some texts which offer support for the ecojustice agenda, and others which people committed to ecojustice should suspect and resist. It is obvious that these different approaches will often disagree about what the biblical texts mean. But it should also be obvious that they disagree because of their different starting points, their different commitments and sources of authority. As we proceed through a series of case studies, looking at a range of biblical texts, we will see more of this diversity of approaches in practice. This will help to indicate what the strengths and weaknesses of each approach might be, and thus help to show what is required of any constructive attempt to develop an ecological reading of the Bible. The case studies will, for obvious reasons, focus largely on the favourite or controversial texts, those most immediately relevant to our topic and concerns. But in the final section of the book, I shall suggest ways in which an ecological hermeneutics might, and must, broaden beyond a narrow textual base and engage in a re-reading of the biblical tradition more generally.

Further reading

Horrell, David G., Hunt, Cherryl and Southgate, Christopher, "Appeals to the Bible in Ecotheology and Environmental Ethics: A Typology of Hermeneutical Stances", *Studies in Christian Ethics* 21 (2008) 219–38.

Conradie, Ernst M., "Towards an Ecological Biblical Hermeneutics: A Review Essay on the Earth Bible Project", *Scriptura* 85 (2004) 123–35.

Habel, Norman C. (ed.), *Readings from the Perspective of Earth* (EB 1; Sheffield: Sheffield Academic Press, 2000).

Habel, Norman C. and Trudinger, Peter (eds), *Exploring Ecological Hermeneutics* (SBL Symposium Series 46; Atlanta: Society of Biblical Literature, 2008).

Beisner, E. Calvin, *Where Garden Meets Wilderness: Evangelical Entry into the Environmental Debate* (Grand Rapids, MI: Acton Institute for the Study of Religion and Liberty/Eerdmans, 1997).

Berry, Sam, *et al.*, *A Christian Approach to the Environment* (The John Ray Initiative, 2005).

Maier, Harry O., "Green Millenialism: American Evangelicals, Environmentalism, and the Book of Revelation", in David G. Horrell, Cherryl Hunt, Christopher Southgate and Francesca Stavrakopoulou (eds), *Ecological Hermeneutics: Biblical, Historical, and Theological Perspectives* (London and New York: T.&T. Clark, forthcoming, January 2010).

Horrell, David G., '*The Green Bible*: A Timely Idea Deeply Flawed', *Expository Times* 121 (forthcoming, January 2010).

Creation Care Websites & Statements, An EarthCare Resource Guide (Chattanooga, TN: EarthCare, 2008), at http://www.earthcareonline.org/creation_care_websites.pdf

Part II

A SURVEY OF SELECTED BIBLICAL TEXTS AND THEIR VARIED INTERPRETATION

Chapter 3

HUMAN DOMINION OVER CREATION?

An overview of Genesis 1–2

The opening words of the Hebrew scriptures, in the first book of the Jewish *Torah* and the Christian Bible, are "in the beginning" (Gen. 1:1). The story of the making of "the heavens and the earth" (ESV), with its canonical position at the opening of the scriptures, has of course been of enormous influence and underpins the Christian doctrine of creation. The story has also long been a focus for controversy and debate, particularly since the findings and theories of modern science began to call into question the value of Genesis 1–2 as any kind of historical or scientific account of the earth's origins. In some Christian circles, more prominent in the USA than in Europe, the creation-evolution debate remains a topic of public disagreement with implications for educational policy. The more recent rise of ecological concerns has brought new challenges and questions to the interpretation of Genesis 1–2.

It has long been recognized that there are two accounts of the making of heaven and earth placed side-by-side in the final form of Genesis: 1:1–2:4a and 2:4b–25 (which continues on into Chapter 3). These two accounts have traditionally been assigned to two different sources, one reflecting priestly interests and convictions (P: 1:1–2:4a) the other the perspective of a so-called Yahwist, given the use of the divine name Yhwh in that source (J: 2:4b–25). Recent scholarship has seriously challenged the cogency of the established four-source theory of the Pentateuch (J, E, D, P), but it is at least clear enough that in Genesis 1 and 2 we have two different accounts of the creation.

The account in Genesis 1 begins with the earth "formless and empty". Then, in response to God's call, "let there be" (*fiat* in the Latin Vulgate), a series of events takes place by which the earth brings forth life. It is important to note how far these primal events are depicted as a process of separating, or ordering – something that probably reflects a priestly concern. There is no hint here of the later doctrine of *creatio ex nihilo* – creation out of nothing. Instead, God's creative work is a matter of bringing order, form and life to what was previously formless. Indeed, some Old Testament texts (e.g. Pss 74:12–17; 89:8–14) seem to depict God's work in creation as a battle with chaos, a *Chaoskampf*, in which God subdues mighty beasts and establishes order. It is hard to see that imagery explicitly in Genesis 1, though some have suggested it might lie in the background (see Fretheim 2005: 43–46).

First to emerge is light, which is separated from darkness to form day and night, each with their allotted time – evening, then morning, as darkness gives way to light, thus forming the first "day" in the six-day story of God's creative activity. The "lights" in the sky – with two "great lights", one for the day, one for the night – appear later, after the land produces vegetation (vv. 14–18). The opening sequence continues with the making of an "expanse" or "canopy" which separates the waters into two, below and above the sky (or "heavens") – a reflection of an ancient worldview in which there are waters beneath and above the sky. The Hebrew word *shamayim* can be translated sky or heaven(s), so we should always be wary assuming the kind of "spiritual" meaning that we might take from the word "heaven". The opening of this account, describing the making of *et ha-shshamayim wᵉet ha-'arets*, is usually translated "the heavens and the earth", but it might also be rendered "the sky and the earth", as Norman Habel suggests (cf. Habel 2000b: 36, 41).

After the water "under the sky" has been gathered into one place, allowing dry ground to appear (vv. 9–10), then life begins to be made: vegetation (vv. 11–12); sea creatures and birds (vv. 20–21), then creatures that live on the land, classified into three broad types: livestock, wild animals, and animals that crawl on the ground (vv. 24–25). The culmination of these creative acts is the making of humanity (*'adam*, the Hebrew word for a human being, which also, of course, becomes the proper name of the first man as the narrative of Genesis continues; vv. 26–30).

Uniquely, humanity – both male and female – is made in the image and likeness of God (vv. 26–27). Like the sea creatures and birds (though not the land-creatures, to whom this is not said), God blesses humanity with the command to "be fruitful and increase" (vv. 22, 28). But humanity also receives a much greater blessing and commission, to "rule" or "have dominion" (Heb verb: *radah*) over all living creatures and to "subdue" (Heb verb: *kabash*) the earth. Strikingly, though, given this mandate to rule, both humans and (land/sky) animals are given (only) plants for food: in other words, the original creation as depicted in Genesis 1 is a herbivorous or vegetarian one. This is a theme we shall encounter again.

A refrain which runs throughout this creation account is God's seeing that what has been made is "good" (vv. 4, 10, 12, 18, 21, 25, 31). Verse 31 sums up this theme with the declaration that "God saw everything that he had made, and behold, it was very good" (v. 31). Interestingly, this is not explicitly said about the making of humanity, nor is it a point that is made in the second creation account in Genesis 2. This declaration may not necessarily mean, in the context of this priestly writing, that the creation is regarded as morally good or perfect in all respects, as, for example, Calvin suggests: "perfectly good … the highest perfection" (Calvin 1965 [1554]: 100). Instead, perhaps, what may be implied is that it is "good for achieving its purpose" (Rogerson 1991: 61; cf. Westermann 1974b: 229), "good" insofar as its harmonious and ordered existence "supported all life forms as God had made them" (Hartley 2000: 50). Gerhard von Rad, who suggests that the declaration "Behold, it was very good" could be "correctly translated 'completely perfect'" goes on to note that this perfection "refers more to the wonderful properness and harmony than to the beauty of the entire cosmos" (von Rad 1963: 59).

The first creation account concludes with the account of God's rest on the seventh day, a story which no doubt serves as an aetiology or "explanation" for the origin and importance of the sabbath, perhaps again reflecting the priestly preoccupations of this version of the story.

The second creation story, which begins in Gen. 2:4b, is very different. The opening of the account lists all the things that had *not* yet appeared – no plants, no rain, no humans (v. 5). The first thing to happen is that a mist (or some kind of flood; the meaning of the Hebrew *'ed* is obscure) comes up from the earth and waters the ground. Interestingly, there is no mention here of God commanding; this water simply arises "from the earth". The first thing God is described as doing is forming the human (*'adam*) from the dust of the ground (*'adamah*). The word play in Hebrew here can hardly be reproduced in English, though Phyllis Trible's phrase "the human from the humus" captures it well (Trible 1993: 42); the human is "an earth creature" (Trible 1978: 77). In the account of Genesis 2, only the human is explicitly said to have had the "breath of life" breathed into him by God; thus he becomes a "living being" (*nefesh chayah*). Nonetheless, the other creatures are described using exactly the same terms: each is also a *nefesh chayah* (2.19; cf. Gen. 7.22, where all creatures on the land are described as those "in whose nostrils was the breath of life", ESV).

The account of Genesis 2 has a more horticultural orientation than Genesis 1, perhaps reflecting the different circles that produced or shaped the various stories. In Genesis 2, the first thing God does with the human is to place him into the garden God has planted in order that he can "work it and keep it" (vv. 8, 15; cf. v. 5). The human is also commanded not to eat from "the tree of the knowledge of good and evil" (v. 17), which, along with the tree of life (v. 9), stands in the middle of the garden.

Another important point in the story is God's decision that the human needs a "helper" (Heb: *'ezer*), and that God will make one for him (v. 18). It is only now that we hear, almost incidentally, that God has already made the animals and birds (v. 19). All of these are brought to the *'adam* to name. This process of naming implies a certain status and power on the part of the human (cf. Mk 5:9). As Claus Westermann comments: "By giving the animals names, the man arranges them in his world" (Westermann 1988: 20). Yet none of these creatures is suitable as a helper; none "corresponds" to the human, or is "like" the *'adam* (as the Septuagint puts it). So the *'adam* is put into a deep sleep and a rib taken out, which God "builds" into a woman. The *'adam* welcomes this new creature, a helper fit for him, as "bone of my bone, and flesh of my flesh" (v. 23). And for the first time in the Old Testament, the names which distinguish man from woman are introduced: she will be called *ishshah*, woman, for she was taken from *ish*, man (2:23; cf. Gen. 1:27, where different words describe humanity as "male and female"). The human, the *'adam*, has been divided into male and female. Again the story serves an aetiological purpose, explaining why it is that an *ish* leaves his father and mother to unite as "one flesh" with an *ishshah*, so providing an influential theological underpinning of the institution of marriage.

The problems of Genesis 1: Readings of recovery

For obvious reasons, these creation stories are of great relevance to any ecological engagement with the Bible: they describe God's making of the earth, and give some sense of the relationships and relative value among the various creatures. Within these stories undoubtedly the most influential and crucial text is the description of the creation of humanity in the priestly account of Genesis 1. In particular, the mandate given to humanity to "rule" the animals and "subdue" the earth (1:26, 28) may be seen as the key biblical text undergirding the kind of damaging anthropocentrism that Lynn White famously saw at the root of our modern ecological crisis (see ch. 1). Among the most prominent themes in discussion has been the range of possible interpretations of this "dominion" text.

Those concerned to find in the Bible positive support for the contemporary ecological agenda, and others who have simply reacted against the Lynn White thesis, have sought, in various ways, to show that this text cannot be held responsible for legitimating any wide-ranging mandate for human exploitation of the earth, nor for its contemporary manifestations in scientific and technological mastery of nature. Nonetheless, this text proves one of the hardest to defend against the criticism that the Bible may generate a view of human superiority and vocation that insufficiently values the rest of the earth community.

Some of the works which defend Gen. 1:26–28 against the kind of criticisms implied by White are concerned to interpret the text in its ancient historical context. An early response to White was made by James Barr (1972), who argued that the Hebrew words used in Gen. 1:26–28 were not as "strong" as had often been suggested, and that the biblical foundations of the doctrine of creation "would tend ... away from a licence to exploit and towards a duty to respect and to protect" (p. 30). More broadly, Barr concludes that "there is much less direct connection between biblical faith and modern science than has been recently believed in some theological currents. The Jewish-Christian doctrine of creation is therefore much less responsible for the ecological crisis than is suggested by arguments such as those of Lynn White" (p. 30). Norbert Lohfink, without any reference to White but engaging with similar views in the German context, argues that the "blessing" of Gen. 1:28 refers to the divine plan for each nation to "take possession of their own regions", and for humans to domesticate animals in a way which establishes a form of peaceful co-existence (Lohfink 1994: 8, 12–13). Since the text has this kind of expansion of human civilization and domestication of animals in view, Lohfink argues, like Barr, that it is inappropriate to use it "to legitimate what humanity has inaugurated in modern times ... The Jewish-Christian doctrine of humanity ... regards human beings very highly, but it would never designate them as absolute rulers of the universe" (p. 17).

Bernhard Anderson highlights the stress in the creation account of Genesis 1 on bringing order; it describes the process by which earth "increasingly becomes an orderly habitation" (Anderson 1984: 158). Anderson agrees that the making of humanity does appear as the crown of the acts of creation, and notes that humans uniquely share the divine image (1.26). Yet, in the "overall pattern of the account ... the emphasis falls not so much on anthropology ... as on ecology, that is, the earthly habitation which human beings share with other forms of 'living being'" (p. 158). Like Lohfink, Anderson suggests that human dominion is connected primarily with the idea of "population growth and diffusion", "the capacity to multiply and fill the earthly *oikos*" (pp. 159–60).

Another strategy is to place this difficult text into its wider literary context. Mark Brett, for example, offers a reading of Genesis 1–2 which suggests that this literary context itself mollifies the problematic implications of 1:26–31 (Brett 2000). Brett, like other writers, stresses how the concerns of the text reflect the ancient agrarian setting: possessing the land and domesticating animals can be seen as essential aspects of sustaining human life in such a setting, and the "dominion" over the animals may be seen as primarily related to real threats posed by wild animals and the desire to control or remove such threats to human wellbeing. With regard to Gen. 1:26–31, Brett, again along with many other writers, notes the use of language which reflects the ideology of kingly rule. Westermann comments that humanity is depicted here as exercising "sovereignty over the rest of creation. The verb used here [*radah*] means 'subjugate', and is used particularly of the rule of kings" (Westermann 1988: 11; cf., e.g., Ps. 110:2). Brett argues that Gen. 1:26–31 can be seen as a *democratization* of this kingly-rule tradition, in that it portrays humanity as a whole as called to rule over the creatures (Brett 2000: 77–78; cf. Lohfink 1994: 4). The text thus represents "a polemical undermining of a role which is otherwise associated primarily with kings ... the democratizing tendency of Gen. 1:27–28 can be seen as anti-monarchic" (Brett 2000: 77). Brett goes on to examine the second creation account (Genesis 2) and sees this account, compared with that in Genesis 1, as more firmly placing human beings in kinship with all other creatures, rather than in a kingly relationship to them (pp. 80–82, etc.); thus, he argues, the editors of Genesis "have produced a text which potentially subverts the 'species supremacy' which lies behind the ecological crisis" (p. 86).

A highly influential approach which attempts to recover from biblical texts such as Gen. 1:28 a message compatible with, and of positive value to, the ecological agenda reinterprets the notion of human dominion in terms of a model of *stewardship*. This approach picks up the use of kingly language in Gen. 1:26–28 and interprets it within the broader treatment of kingship in the Old Testament. Kingly rule, it is argued, was not about domination and exploitation, at least in terms of the biblical "ideal". Westermann, for example, writing on Gen. 1:26–31, comments that "[a]ccording to the ancient view ... there is no suggestion of exploitation; on the contrary, the king is personally responsible for the well-being and prosperity of those he rules. His rule serves the well-being of his subjects" (1988: 11). From this perspective, the language of rule and dominion can be read as implying a responsibility on the part of humans. Brennan Hill puts the point forcefully: "humans were created to act nobly in the place of the Creator ... this leaves no room for 'lording over' or 'mastering' humans or any other living things. Tragically, the passage has all too often been distorted and used to justify the domination of both human beings and nature" (Hill 1998: 38).

Treatments aiming to retrieve a positive sense of the relationship between humanity and the rest of creation outlined in Gen. 1:28 also highlight the repeated declarations earlier in Genesis 1, that creation is valuable, is "good" in God's sight even before humans appear (vv. 10, 12, 18, 21, 25, 31; Osborn 1993: 86). Also important to developing the theme of stewardship is the imagery of Genesis 2, where the human is placed in the garden "to till and keep it" (Gen. 2:15). Indeed, the "stewardship" model of humanity's relationship to the earth has become a central plank in many attempts to construct a biblical environmental ethic (see, e.g., Wilkinson *et al.* 1980; Granberg-Michaelson 1987b; Hall 1990 [1982]) and, more recently, in a realignment of major evangelical leaders and bodies behind a more environmentally-conscious vision of Christian responsibility, as expressed, e.g., in "An Evangelical Declaration on the Care of Creation" (1994 [in Berry 2000: 17–22]) and the Evangelical Climate Initiative (2006). A similar stance is reflected in *The Green Bible*, published in 2008 (for a critique, see Horrell forthcoming b).

The reading strategy at work here can be related to the typology presented in Chapter 2: evangelicals who are committed to the environmental agenda need to show how the Bible can be read in an ecologically positive way, and need to defend texts like Gen. 1:26–28 against the charge that they legitimate aggressive human domination of the earth.

Yet questions have been raised about the value of the stewardship model for an environmental ethic (see, e.g., Palmer 1992; Bauckham 2000; Southgate 2006). While it may represent an implicit biblical model of the relationship between king and people (interpreted, it might be added, in a rather idealistic, even naïve, way), it may be questioned whether it is actually a biblical image specifically of the relationship of humans to creation, which is the crucial point for those who promote environmental stewardship as a Bible-based model of care for creation. As John Reumann points out, stewardship terminology is actually used rather little in the Bible (Reumann 1992: 7): "[t]here are virtually no Old Testament roots for what the New Testament and Church Fathers did with the *oikonomia* [stewardship] theme" (p. 16) and "[i]t cannot be claimed that *oikonomia* constitutes a major New Testament theme" (p. 18). Moreover, where this does occur, it does not relate to human responsibility for non-human creation. Second, as Clare Palmer suggests, it is an image primarily based on financial and other forms of delegated responsibility and which contains various negative implications; the steward is someone given charge of the owner's property (see, e.g., Luke 16:1–8). "The political message encoded in stewardship", Palmer argues, "is one of power and oppression; of server and served" (Palmer 1992: 76). Moreover, various ecologically problematic assumptions seem to underlie the concept: "a strong sense of humanity's separation from the rest of the world"; the idea "that the natural world is a human resource, that humans are really in control of nature, that nature is dependent on humanity for its management" (pp. 77–78). In short, according to Palmer, it amounts to an anthropocentric and patronizing ethic (pp. 81–84). Richard Bauckham similarly asks whether:

> the image of stewardship is still too freighted with the baggage of the modern project of technological domination of nature. Can we entirely free it of the implication that nature is always better off when managed by us, that nature needs our benevolent intrusions, that it is our job to turn the whole world into a well-tended garden inhabited by well-cared-for pets? (Bauckham 2002a: 172)

Another response to the argument that Genesis 1–2, and specifically 1:26–28, legitimizes human domination of the earth, of the kind that has fostered the modern scientific and technological project of mastering nature, is to insist that such an ideology is not so much a product of the text itself as of much later historical developments. This is precisely the argument, explicitly developed in response to White's charges, in Richard Bauckham's essay on "Human Authority in Creation" (Bauckham 2002a: 128–77; see also Harrison 1999, with similar conclusions).

Genesis 1:26–28 was reinterpreted through a framework very different from that which the text itself represents, Bauckham suggests, when it was read by early Christian interpreters through the lens of Greek philosophy. From this source came ideas of human uniqueness and superiority over nature, a utilitarian understanding of the world, a view of dominion as "the right to make use of all creatures for human benefit" (p. 135), a strongly hierarchical view of the world, and a distinction between humans as rational and animals as irrational, and therefore not needing or deserving considerations of justice (pp. 133–38).

Yet even this view, prevalent in the medieval period, was not, Bauckham argues, "sufficient to authorise ... the modern project of technological domination of nature" (p. 141). This was because, despite this view of human supremacy, "dominion was understood as a static fact, not a mandate for extension, and the world was understood as created ready and adapted to human use, not requiring large-scale technological modification" (p. 141). This early interpretation of the Genesis mandate is thus to be sharply distinguished "from the interpretation of the dominion that accompanied the rise of the modern project of technological domination of nature" (p. 141).

Moreover, the view of human dominion in this period was set firmly within a *theocentric* perspective: humanity's "vertical" position of dominance over nature was sharply qualified by a sense of its "horizontal" relationship with all creatures who relate to the Creator (pp. 141–42). These important qualifications fell away with the Renaissance interpretation of human dominion: "When any sense of the value of creation for God and of a common creatureliness in which humans share was lost, the idea of human dominion would acquire quite new significance" (p. 142).

Thus Bauckham traces the birth of "the modern project of unlimited domination of nature" to sixteenth-century Renaissance humanism, in which appeals to Gen. 1:26–28, etc. were not infrequently found. "The attitudes that have led to the contemporary ecological crisis can be traced back to this source, but no further" (p. 157). The ideological underpinnings of this project developed further with Francis Bacon (1561–1626), one of the founding figures of modern science. "Central to Bacon's vision of scientific progress is his understanding of the goal of science as the implementation of the God-given human dominion over nature, which Bacon himself presents as the meaning of Genesis 1:28" (p. 159). Hence, dominion comes to be seen not as a static description of what is the case, but rather as a "historical task" (p. 160). Humans come to "play the role of God in relation to the world" (p. 167). So, according to Bauckham:

> the ideological roots of the modern Western project of aggressive domination of nature are to be found in a traditional interpretation of the human dominion over nature that drew on Greek rather than biblical sources and was subsequently, in the Renaissance, removed from its broader context in a Christian understanding of creation. (p. 165)

In essence, the claim here is that the problem lies not with the biblical text but only with the ways it was misinterpreted, first through the lens of essentially non-biblical Greek ideas and then much later in the context of Renaissance views of human possibilities and progress. Indeed, Bauckham suggests, biblical themes such as the placing of humanity *within* the community of creation, and the praise of God by all creation, offer the basis for a positive environmental ethic and a theological framework within which dominion can be much more positively interpreted (see Bauckham 2002a: 176–77; Bauckham 2002b).

Other studies of the history of interpretation of Gen: 1:26–28 too have concluded that, in the pre-modern period, there was no particular interest in interpreting the text as a mandate for aggressive domination of nature for human ends. Only when science and technology began to make such aims conceivable, it seems, did that particular kind of view of human dominion begin to emerge (see Baranzke and Lamberty-Zielinski 1995; Harrison 1999). However, questions remain – to which we will return below – concerning the extent to which such conclusions resolve the difficulties of Gen. 1:26–28 and its (ongoing) influence.

Resistant readings of Gen. 1:26–28

While many biblical scholars and theologians have thus sought to defend Gen. 1:26–28 against the criticisms levelled at it by those following Lynn White, others have taken a different stance. Some members of the Earth Bible Team, committed to reading biblical texts in the light of ecojustice principles (see ch. 2), find this Genesis text guilty as charged. Norman Habel, main editor of the Earth Bible series, is concerned to confront what he regards as the naïve assumption evident in many works of ecotheology "that the Bible is environmentally friendly" (Habel 2000a: 30). He argues, for example, that Gen. 1:26–28 cannot be read in a positive, earth-friendly way:

> The verb *kabash* ("to subdue") not only confirms the status of humans as having power over Earth; it also points to harsh control. Subduing the land meant crushing opposing forces. There is nothing gentle about *kabash* ...
> The orientation of the human story (Gen. 1:26–28) is overtly hierarchical: humans are authorized to rule other creatures and to subdue Earth. (Habel 2000b: 46–47)

For Habel, the story of the making of humanity (Gen. 1:26–31) disrupts and conflicts with the story of the making of Earth – capitalized as a character by Habel (Gen. 1:1–25). In the opening verses of Genesis, life emerges through a fruitful collaboration between God and Earth; here the Earth is a partner in the story, a willing actor in the generation of living things. With the creation of humanity, however, that partnership is changed; now Earth is to be dominated and ruled from above by humanity. Reading "from the perspective of Earth" – a central concern of the Earth Bible series – this is a damaging and unfortunate story, which does not support the kind of ecojustice principles to which the Team is committed (see also Habel 2001a: 180–84).

Another writer in the series, Howard Wallace, is similarly unconvinced by attempts to recover a positive reading of Gen. 1:28: "The roots of any modern ecological problems to which an emphasis on Gen. 1:28 and human domination of creation has contributed, would thus seem to be embedded in the biblical text itself and its own internal means of interpretation" (Wallace 2000: 56). In other words, Wallace essentially sides with White insofar as Gen. 1:26–28 is indeed seen as implicated in causing the ecological problems that have stemmed from aggressive human exploitation of the earth.

The idea that humanity is made in the image of God, despite its huge influence, is actually rather rare in the Old Testament, found primarily in these opening chapters of Genesis (1:26–27; 5:3; 9:6; cf. Wisd 2:23). The other place in the Old Testament where a similar idea is expressed, linked with a strong statement about humanity's dominion over the earth, is in Psalm 8 (cf. Hill 1998: 37): "Yet you have made them [human beings] a little lower than God [Heb *'elohim*], and crowned them with glory and honour. You have given them dominion over the works of your hands; you have put all things under their feet" (Ps. 8:5–6). Keith Carley, also writing in the Earth Bible series, offers a similarly critical treatment of this text. According to Carley, this Psalm represents "an apology for human domination" which does not conform to the ecojustice principles. The model of domination which the Psalm presents and legitimizes – "a classic expression", Carley suggests, "of the dominating male ego" – has been a cause of suffering for too long, and needs to be rejected (Carley 2000: 122).

Following the classification of different reading strategies presented in Chapter 2, and specifically recalling the two types of "resistance", it can be seen that these writers represent a reading of the text which exposes and resists what is taken to be its negative impact, given a commitment to principles of ecojustice. The other type of resistance is also evident in some Christian writing, namely a resistance to the modern environmental agenda. Calvin Beisner, for example, agrees with Habel and others that the Hebrew words *kabash* ("subdue") and *radah* ("rule") convey "strong, forceful subjugation" (Beisner 1997: 103; cf. 178 n. 21). In other words, Beisner agrees that Gen. 1:26–28 (among other texts) does place humanity in a position of authority over the earth. But for Beisner this is not a problem;

on the contrary, it is an important element of the biblical Christian worldview. Beisner sees human subjugation of nature as a crucial task, restoring and redeeming nature from its curse, turning it from wilderness into garden so that it might "meet man's needs – and the needs of other creatures as well – more fully than it naturally would" (p. 104). While environmentalists celebrate the beauty of wildernesses and seek to protect them, Beisner points to the biblical texts that depict wilderness as a sign of God's curse (pp. 117–28). Insofar as the environmental movement rejects this biblical doctrine of God-given human dominion, it should itself, Beisner suggests, be rejected as un-Christian.

Conclusion

There have been a variety of readings of Genesis 1–2, and specifically of Gen. 1:26–28, in response to the kind of critical issues opened up especially by White's classic article. Some writers, as we have seen, argue that the text cannot originally have meant anything like what White's thesis takes it to mean. Others develop a "stewardship" reading of the imagery of dominion, insisting that any use of it to legitimate human exploitation of the earth is a "distortion" of its true meaning (Hill 1998: 38, 42). Yet others, such as Habel, insist that the crucial dominion text cannot be so easily brought into congruity with an ecological perspective. Indeed, it should be clear that the text is at least open to a range of readings, and its language of rule and dominion can certainly imply ruthless and forceful domination as well as more benevolent forms of authority. Gen. 1:26–28 cannot easily be rescued or recovered for an environmental biblical theology.

Texts such as Gen. 1:26–28 are, always and inevitably, open to a range of different readings. Competing readings – mandate for human domination, or call to responsible stewardship? – are often presented as arguments about the "real" meaning of the text in its original historical context. Bauckham's argument, in a sense, is concerned to show that ecologically damaging attitudes stemmed from Renaissance ideas and cannot be traced back to the text itself. Yet the biblical texts can and do sustain a variety of readings, readings which arise from and are shaped by changing historical circumstances and specific readerly locations. Historical studies are valuable in highlighting the original context of the text, thus showing how its concerns and foci were very different from those of the later contexts in which it has been interpreted. Yet debates about different interpretations cannot be resolved simply by trying to determine the original meaning or intention of the text, nor by showing how certain interpretations reflect the influence of later ideological frameworks, since all interpretations are, in various ways, products of a particular set of historical, ideological, theological and ethical convictions.

The Baconian interpretation of Gen. 1:26–28 as a mandate for the active implementation of a programme of human dominion arose within a context of new discovery and immense optimism about the possibilities of science. The evangelical interpretation of Gen. 1:26–28 as a call for responsible stewardship of nature arises within a context of growing awareness of the negative impact of human activity on the planet's ecosystems, and a more chastened sense of the limits and dangers – as well as the positive benefits – of science. Neither interpretation can simply be declared a false reading of this text. Or, put differently, both interpretations are, in a sense, "distortions" of the text, since both make of it something rather different from what its own content and context imply.

Since the text can thus be read and appropriated in various ways, a crucial question rapidly emerges: Why should we read the text one way rather than another; why we should view it through one interpretative lens rather than a different one? The alternatives are partly to be judged through careful exegesis and historical study, since these can help us to see how some readings simply represent implausible ways to construe the Hebrew text. Yet an equally crucial part of the task is to argue, on theological and ethical grounds, and given the contemporary context we inhabit, why one approach is better than another. Also important is to question which texts and images should be of central influence, and which should be marginalized. Genesis 1 has, for various reasons, exerted huge influence on the Christian doctrine of creation and of humanity – uniquely made in the image of God. In an age dominated by ecological concerns and problems, other texts might offer more fruitful resources and might have a claim to be brought to the centre of a biblical theology.

The opening chapters of Genesis, then, offer an ambivalent legacy to an environmental reading of the Bible. Some aspects of their content may be important to an ecological theology (such as the insistence on the goodness of all creation) or suggestive for contemporary ethics (such as the depiction of a non-violent, vegetarian creation). But other aspects, especially in the crucial dominion text (Gen. 1:26–28), are at least open to a reading which supports a sense of humanity's unique value and right to use the planet for its benefit. Right at the outset of our studies of biblical texts, then, we see that it is not easy to sustain the claim that the Bible has a consistent or obviously "green" message. Rather, there are complex questions about how to interpret and to weigh various ambivalent texts and how to deal constructively with their equally ambivalent legacies.

Further reading

Rogerson, John W., *Genesis 1–11* (OTG; Sheffield: Sheffield Academic Press, 1991).

——, "The Creation Stories: Their Ecological Potential and Problems", in David G. Horrell, Cherryl Hunt, Christopher Southgate and Francesca Stavrakopoulou (eds), *Ecological Hermeneutics: Biblical, Historical, and Theological Perspectives* (London and New York: T. & T. Clark, forthcoming).

Westermann, Claus, *Creation* (London: SPCK, 1974).

Habel, Norman C. and Wurst, Shirley (eds), *The Earth Story in Genesis* (EB 2; Sheffield: Sheffield Academic Press, 2000).

Bauckham, Richard J., *God and the Crisis of Freedom: Biblical and Contemporary Perspectives* (Louisville, KY/London: Westminster John Knox, 2002), 128–77.

Harrison, Peter, "Subduing the Earth: Genesis 1, Early Modern Science, and the Exploitation of Nature", *Journal of Religion* 79 (1999) 86–109.

Berry, R. J. (ed.), *The Care of Creation* (Leicester: IVP, 2000).

—— (ed.), *Environmental Stewardship: Critical Perspectives, Past and Present* (London and New York: T. & T. Clark, 2006).

Chapter 4

THE "FALL" AND THE FLOOD: A COVENANT WITH ALL
THE EARTH

A curse on the ground: Human disobedience and its consequences

In the Christian tradition, the story told in Genesis 3, after the two accounts of creation in the opening chapters, is regarded as the story of the Fall. This is a crucial moment, a misstep in the history of humankind, when through Adam's (and Eve's) disobedience sin enters the world and with it the sentence of condemnation and death. Henceforth, humans are marked by the propensity to sin, enslaved under its power. Adam's "original sin" defines the character and fate of the human race, which stands in need of redemption.

It is important to note at the outset of this chapter, then, that this is not exactly how the narrative of Genesis 3 presents things, and that the focus on the Fall as a defining moment in the history of humankind is not found in the Hebrew scriptures. There are no direct references to Genesis 3 elsewhere in the Old Testament (Bruggemann 1982: 41; Fretheim 2005: 321, n. 1), though there are some close parallels in Ezek. 28:11–19; this oracle against the king of Tyre describes him as blameless in Eden (vv. 12–15), until unrighteousness was found in him (vv. 15–19; see Rogerson 1991: 65–66). As Claus Westermann puts it: "The Old Testament knows nothing of a narrative which says that man sank into a state of corruption, that from that moment on he was 'fallen man'" (Westermann 1974a: 89). Walter Brueggemann comments similarly: "The text is commonly treated as the account of '*the fall*'. Nothing could be more remote from the narrative itself ... In general, the Old Testament does not assume such a 'fall'" (Brueggemann 1982: 41). Later Jewish literature did begin to develop this idea, seeing Adam and/or Eve as the original sinner(s), through whom the universal disease of sin and the consequent punishment of death entered the world. For example, the *Wisdom of Solomon* (probably first century BCE) states that "through the devil's envy death entered the world"

(Wisd. 2:24, NRSV), while *Sirach* puts the blame on the woman: "From a woman sin had its beginning, and because of her we all die" (Sir. 25:24, NRSV). A focus on Adam comes out particularly in 4 Ezra (probably late first century CE):

> And you laid upon him [Adam] one commandment of yours; but he transgressed it, and immediately you appointed death for him and for his descendants (3.7) ... For the first Adam, burdened with an evil heart, transgressed and was overcome, as were also all who were descended from him. Thus the disease became permanent (3:21–22) ... O Adam, what have you done? For though it was you who sinned, the fall was not yours alone, but ours also who are your descendants. (4 Ezra 7:118, NRSV)

But it is in the Christian tradition, and especially with Paul, whose influence is then decisive, that the narrative of Genesis 3 assumes central doctrinal significance as the point from which sin and death came to affect all humanity, through the representative and original human, Adam. For Paul, Adam forms an important "type" of Christ. Both are figures whose actions affected and encompassed all humanity, one for ill, the other for good:

> Therefore, just as sin came into the world through one man, and death came through sin, and so death spread to all because all have sinned – sin was indeed in the world before the law, but sin is not reckoned when there is no law. Yet death exercised dominion from Adam to Moses, even over those whose sins were not like the transgression of Adam, who is a type of the one who was to come. But the free gift is not like the trespass. For if the many died through the one man's trespass, much more surely have the grace of God and the free gift in the grace of the one man, Jesus Christ, abounded for the many. (Rom. 5:12–15, NRSV)

Given this weighty and influential tradition of interpretation, it is important to try to attend afresh to the story of Genesis 3, and to consider what ecological relevance and implications the passage might have. Here, and throughout this chapter, I will not be concerned with source-critical questions regarding these chapters of Genesis – for example, on the possible division of the Flood-story into J and P accounts (see Rogerson 1991: 70–72) – but will read the narratives as found in their final form.

The story in Genesis 3 takes its cue from the commandment to the human (*ha-'adam*) given in Gen. 2:17, not to eat from the tree of the knowledge of good and evil. The serpent, who opens the dialogue with the woman in 3:1, is described as the most shrewd or crafty of the animals (3:1; not "wild" animals, as the NRSV and NIV have it, but "beasts of the field", as in 2:19–20). It is important to note that this description is not necessarily negative, and certainly does not depict the snake as evil, despite, once again, a long tradition identifying the serpent with Satan or the Devil (cf. Fretheim 2005: 73). In Prov. 12:23, for example, the same adjective (Heb *'arum*) is used to mean prudent or sensible, and the LXX rendering of Gen. 3:1 may also be taken in the sense of wise or prudent (Gk *phronimōtatos*). Indeed, the serpent appears to tell the woman the truth – that eating the fruit will not lead to death, but to knowledge of good and evil (3:4-5) – a truth that God confirms in 3:22. Since the humans now have become like gods, knowing good and evil, they must be prevented from also eating from the tree of life, which would grant them the divine quality of immortality. One of the themes at work in this text seems to be that of maintaining the distinction between God/gods and humans. The disobedience of the man and the woman to God's command, intended to keep them from acquiring the discernment that belongs to the divine realm, leads to their expulsion from the Garden, in order to keep them away from the tree of life (3:22–24).

A key passage within this chapter of Genesis is 3:14–19, where God pronounces judgement consequent upon this action: a curse on the serpent and on the ground, and implications (though no curse, explicitly) for the woman and the man. Although the text is formulated as a divine curse, where God brings about certain consequences ("I will put enmity ... I will greatly increase your pains"), it is probably right, as a number of scholars have argued, to see it also as a reflection of what life then was like, with the brute realities of hardship, suffering and danger. "Every aspect of creaturely life is touched: marriage and sexuality; work and food; birth and death" (Fretheim 2005: 76). The enmity which God introduces between humans and snakes, for example, provides a kind of mythological explanation, an aetiology, for the experience of people who found poisonous snakes a threat, and who would therefore doubtless protect themselves by striking or squashing snakes when they encountered them. God's pronouncement also "explains" why the processes of childbirth are painful, and why women are subjected to the rule of their husbands (3:16). This last phrase, of course, constitutes a particularly difficult and much discussed text: for some, it gives a divine mandate to the subordination of the woman to her husband in marriage; others point out that this situation is a consequence of disobedience and the disruption of relationships, not a divinely established norm. As Westermann comments:

> Presuming that the pronouncements of punishment over the serpent, the woman, and the man do not lay down any norms, but intend to explain the situation which the writer faced, then the verse which says that man should

be the lord of woman should not be regarded as an eternally valid norm. It
describes life as it then was. (Westermann 1974a: 101)

Most interesting from an ecological perspective, though, is the curse
pronounced on the ground (referred to again in Gen 5:29 and 8:21). Once
again, while this is presented as a divine curse which changes the character
of the human-land relationship, it is probably right to see it as a realistic
reflection of the hardships and challenges facing those who sustained their
existence through their toil in the hilly lands of the region. While Hermann
Gunkel influentially suggested that these words presented "an extremely
pessimistic view of human life and of agriculture" (quoted in Westermann
1974a: 102) it is more likely that they are simply reflective of life as it was
experienced. As Shirley Wurst comments, following Carol Meyers, "life in
'the land of milk and honey' was arduous and back-breaking. The soil was
poor, the rainfall low and unpredictable, and much sweat was expended in
eking a living from the soil … The man's predicament, like the woman's,
reflects the reality of life in that period" (Wurst 2000: 97). Westermann
draws a broader and parabolic meaning from the text:

> man's work is always in some way tied up with toil and effort; every area of
> work throws up its thorns and thistles which cannot be avoided; every
> worthwhile accomplishment demands sweat. Acknowledgment and acceptance
> of this fact have nothing to do with pessimism. It is sober realism which
> protects work from any dangerous idealizing. (Westermann 1974a: 102)

Also notable in the curse on the ground is the reaffirmation of the human's
earthy character. As we noted in the previous chapter, the Hebrew words
make clear the intimate connection between the human and the earth:
'*adam* from the '*adamah*. Adam is reminded that he was made from the
ground ('*adamah*) and, composed of dust ('*apar*), will return to dust. This
reminder of human mortality is often taken to indicate that the sentence
of death has indeed been passed because of Adam's sin – as in the later
Jewish and especially Christian interpretations we noted above. But
the text here makes no mention of death as such, nor is there any
reference back to the prohibition and threat of 2:17. Moreover, in 3:22 the
implication is that the humans still have the possibility of living for ever
(cf. Fretheim 2005: 76). What the text does more clearly imply is the strong
interconnectedness of humanity and the earth – interconnectedness being
one of the ecojustice principles adopted by the Earth Bible Team (see p. 14
above). What is more, "[i]n an interesting subtle twist, the snake perhaps
has the last laugh – the dust it is forced to eat is ultimately what humans
are reduced to, in the cycle of mortality" (Wurst 2000: 95). This irony is

thus a further illustration of "the connections the text inscribes between humans and the ground and other living creatures; in this text the Earth community is indissolubly linked by their common origins – they all come from the ground" (Wurst 2000: 89).

Yet an ecojustice reading of this text, such as presented by Wurst (2000), will also note the obvious injustice in the story: the earth is subjected to a curse, despite having played no apparent part in the tale of disobedience. For Wurst this shows how the ground, like a good mother, the Earth-mother, willingly takes her children's punishment upon herself: "The *adamah* asks to take the brunt of the 'curse' on herself, and diminishes the ripples, by grounding the curse in herself. God agrees. The ground, like other mothers in Genesis, wears the curse of her children's destructive behaviour" (p. 100). However, this imaginative reading, thought-provoking though it is, finds little explicit anchor in the text. There is no hint that the ground has any say whatsoever in the decision to pronounce the curse, no hint of its willingness or otherwise to receive this punishment. Moreover, if the "curse" on the ground effectively describes ground "as we know it" (Wurst 2000: 101), reflecting the realities of agricultural life in the author's time and place, then the text is best seen as offering some kind of "explanation" for these harsh realities. Nonetheless, the motifs of interconnectedness (of humans, animals and the earth) and of curse on the land (because of human action) do invite contemporary ecological reflection: "As ecologists have demonstrated, the ground and other members of the Earth community are still bearing the curse-consequences of human actions!" (Wurst 2000: 101). Furthermore, as we shall see again in other contexts (chs 8–9), there are a variety of ancient traditions that see both human degradation and human flourishing as reflected in, and intimately connected to, either degradation or flourishing of the land. This is clearly an anthropocentric picture, as is that of Genesis 3, but it offers an ecologically relevant theme in its drawing of a tight connection between humanity and the earth, stressing that the consequences of human action, like the disobedience of Adam and Eve, have an impact on the whole earth community, for good or ill.

Finally, despite the fact that this description of life after the act of disobedience is a "realistic" one, depicting life as it was then experienced, we should also note that the text implies a conviction that this is a disrupted and distorted existence, shaped by enmity and curse. As we shall see next, this narrative of disruption and corruption continues into the following chapters of Genesis. But such a depiction of "life as it is" also implies that the producers of these stories believed that this state of affairs, with its hardships and sufferings, was not the way it was meant to be, and could dream of an existence that was otherwise.

The spread of corruption and the Flood

While the story of Genesis 3 is hardly that of "the Fall" as traditionally understood, it is perhaps not inappropriate to regard it as depicting some kind of fall (cf. Fretheim 2005: 71): humanity's disobedience not only leads to the curse, and to expulsion from the Garden, but also to an ongoing narrative in which corruption and violence seem henceforth to spread. Ironically, as humanity fulfils the divine imperative to "be fruitful and multiply" (Gen. 1:28), so the scale of the problem grows; human growth and development, the text hints, is at least ambivalent in its impact. "Progress in civilization is always accompanied by progress in sin [cf. Gen. 4:7] and its effects, so that 'progress' becomes an ambiguous reality within God's world" (Fretheim 2005: 79). So, in Gen. 4:1–16, we have the famous murder of Abel by his brother Cain (later involved in urban development, 4:17). Cain's descendant Lamech is guilty of even greater violence (Gen. 4:23–24). An enigmatic but influential story in this narrative of human development appears in 6:1–4, where, with growing numbers of humans on the earth, the "sons of God", divine or angelic figures, marry "the daughters of humankind" (*bᵉnot ha-'adam*), that is, human women. They apparently (though this is not quite explicit in the text) produce giant offspring, known as the Nephilim (cf. Westermann 1988: 44–45). Although their actions are not explicitly labelled a wrongdoing, Jewish and Christian tradition, in which this story was much reflected on, certainly saw this as a significant moment of transgression and rebellion, a crossing of the boundary between heaven and earth, divine and human (see *1 Enoch* 6–10; 2 Pet. 2:4; Jude 6). Indeed, some censure of this action is implied in v. 3, where God announces that the human's lifespan will be limited to 120 years. This, combined with the accounts of lifespans in Genesis 5 and 11:10–26 (short, apparently, by comparison with other ancient Near Eastern lists; so Fretheim 2005: 79), suggests that "diminishing age spans probably depict the debilitating effects of sin over time" (Fretheim 2005: 78). Indeed, the narrative of Gen. 6:1–4 introduces a section in which the corruption not only increases but also spreads to the whole created order.

It is clear that, for the narrator, human wickedness remains at the centre of the picture. Once again, this is an anthropocentric picture, albeit a strongly negative one: "The LORD saw that the wickedness of the human (*ha-'adam*) was great in the earth (*ba-'arets*), and that every inclination of the thoughts of his heart was only evil all the time" (Gen. 6:5). Statements to this effect frame the Flood narrative which begins at this point (see also 8:21), where God decides to wipe humanity from the earth (6:7). But despite this focus on human wickedness, the scope of corruption is evidently felt to be cosmic and universal. Perhaps it is the serpent's action (possibly as a representative of the animal realm) and the action of the "sons of God" which combine to inject an initial sense that corruption has spread beyond the human species. Certainly, God's decision to wipe humanity from the earth is immediately expanded to include "animals [or cattle; Heb *b*e*hemah*] and creeping things and flying creatures", all of which God is sorry to have made (6:7). And the following verses clearly depict the whole earth, and "all flesh" within it, as having become corrupt (6:11–13). While some have argued that the phrase "all flesh" (Heb *kol-basar*) might refer only to humans, "[m]ost commentators recognize that 'all flesh' here and throughout the flood story (cf. 6:19; 7:16; 8:17; 9:16) includes both man and the animals" (Wenham 1987: 171). Indeed, this phrase is repeated a number of times throughout this section of the story, and in some places very clearly seems to encompass all living creatures (Gen. 6:17, 19; 7:16, 21; 8:17).

It is difficult to know what sense we can make of the notion that animals, reptiles and birds – let alone the earth as a whole – might be morally corrupt and wicked. But this is clearly a concept meaningful to the authors/producers of the Hebrew Bible: as well as here in Gen. 6–8, in Isa. 24:20 the "earth" (*'erets*) is depicted as guilty of transgression, while in Jonah the animals of Nineveh join in the acts of repentance (Jon. 3:7–8) and are noticed as of worth by God (4:11). Indeed, as the depictions of both the original creation (Gen. 1:29–30; see ch. 3 above) and the eschatological new creation (see ch. 8 below) show, the violence and predation among animals as well as humans was seen as less than ideal, as a state of affairs that might one day be rectified. Yet with our scientifically informed worldview, it is hard to conceptualize any way in which a sparrow or an earthworm, not to mention a river-bank or woodland, might be wicked. Certainly, since Darwin, it is difficult, theologically as well as scientifically, to imagine any kind of primaeval "fall", difficult enough in the case of humans, and more difficult still in the case of other animals or creation as a whole, since the processes which have entailed suffering, violence and predation have always been intrinsic and essential to the means through which life in all its richness and beauty developed (see Southgate 2008b; ch. 8 below). There is also, of course, the theological difficulty of attributing to God an act of the most drastic and comprehensive ecological destruction imaginable, wiping almost all living things from the earth in an attempt to cleanse it of corruption.

Yet again, despite the difficulties, there are points about this ancient mythological worldview that inspire ecological reflection. One obvious point is that this notion of universal corruption once more underlines the interconnectedness of humanity and the rest of the earth community. As Westermann comments, in relation to the story of Genesis 3: "when the serpent shares in the punishment, then this is an indication that man and the rest of Creation are drawn into a common relationship which is seen in the 'groaning of all creation' [cf. Rom. 8:19–23; ch. 7 below] ... The fact of suffering ... is not limited to man; it belongs to the whole of Creation" (Westermann 1974a: 99–100). What this sense of shared suffering also implies as its positive corollary is that any redemption from this less-than-ideal state of affairs must also encompass the whole earth and all its creatures. Humanity stands at the centre of the picture, whether we like it or not, but humanity's corruption and redemption are intrinsically bound up with the corruption and redemption of all the earth. In a sense, the Flood narrative stands as a paradigm and parable of this point, for righteous Noah and his family are not saved alone, but along with (and taking responsibility for) representatives of all living creatures (6:19–21; 7:2–3, 8–9, 14–16, etc.). Indeed, albeit in still ambivalent and problematic ways, God's speech to Noah after the Flood embodies this ecologically significant conviction.

After the Flood: The covenant with all the earth

A turning point in the Flood narrative comes at Gen. 8:1, where God "remembers". Brueggemann draws attention to this turning point in summary terms: "God remembered Noah. God remembered" (1982: 85). But as John Olley points out (Olley 2000: 137), what Brueggemann (and other commentators) fail sufficiently to note is that the animals in the ark are equally "remembered" by God (8:1; cf. also 9:15). God therefore sends a wind to begin to dry up the waters, and eventually the ark comes to rest on dry ground. Noah sacrifices some animals, and the "pleasing aroma" causes God to promise "never again" to "curse the ground because of humankind ... nor will I ever again destroy every living creature as I have done" (Gen. 8:21, NRSV).

There follows an important and extended speech of God, addressed to Noah and his sons, which falls into two parts: 9:1–7 and 9:8–17. In the first part, the blessing of Gen. 1:28, to "be fruitful and increase", is the framing idea, both opening and closing this section (9:1, 7). This is a cue for the subsequent chapters of the narrative, which continue to tell the story of human expansion and its consequent risks, culminating in the story of the Tower of Babel, when God once again acts to rein in human potential and ambition (Gen. 11:1–9). It should also be noted, though, that this blessing is also extended to the animals in 8:17: they are to be brought out of the ark so that they can "be fruitful and increase" on the earth.

The reiteration of the blessing from Gen. 1:28 in Gen. 9:1 and 7 does not directly repeat the mandate to subdue and rule over the animals. This is not, however, an indication of a more egalitarian and harmonious relationship between humanity and the animals. On the contrary, "fear and dread" now characterizes the stance towards humanity of all the living creatures on the earth – including not only those preserved in the ark, but fish too (9:2). As Olley shows, "fear" (*morah*) and "dread" (*chat*) "are very strong words" which most often "occur in military settings" (Olley 2000: 135; cf. Deut. 11:25; 31:8; Wenham 1987: 192). Why this fear and dread? It is less likely a product of the Flood experience than a reflection of "the animosity between man and the animal world that followed the fall" (Wenham 1987: 192). In other words, humanity's rule over the animals is still presumed, but now made more fearful due to the enmity and disruption injected into previously harmonious relationships: "For subjects to be 'afraid and terrified' is not right! It is a sign that there is something terribly (literally) wrong in the relationship" (Olley 2000: 135). Or, as Fretheim suggests, "[t]he basic creational order still remains, but the dominion charge is complicated by sin and its effects" (2005: 84).

Indeed, in contrast to the herbivorous/vegetarian diet described in Gen. 1:29–30, now the assertion of fear and dread is immediately followed by a permission to human beings to eat "everything that lives and moves" for food (note the emphatic repetition of the idea that God gives all these creatures into humanity's hands in 9:2–3). This unrestricted permission is, however, qualified by the prohibition against eating meat with its "life-blood" still in it (v. 4). Given the context in which this occurs, it seems most plausible to see this as a further indication that this situation, and the human-animal relationship it implies, is less than ideal (cf. Olley 2000: 134). Animals may certainly be eaten, and this inevitably involves shedding their blood, literally or metaphorically, depending on how they are killed, but their blood is not to be consumed, for this is a symbol of their very life, which has been taken.

The motif of the life-blood forms the link into the following statements, which concern the shedding of human blood (vv. 5–6). Any animal, or any human, who sheds the blood of another human, will be held accountable. Strikingly, animals as well as humans bear a moral responsibility in this regard – a further, if again enigmatic, indication of an inclusion of animals within the moral community – but it is only the killing of humans that is prohibited. Once again, the ancient context shapes the concerns of the text: the biblical writers lived with an awareness of the threat to humans from wild animals in a way very different from the experience of modern Western interpreters. Even in the sixteenth century, Calvin could comment on Gen. 9:2 that God "promises that the same dominion shall continue. We see indeed that wild beasts rush violently upon men, and rend and tear many of them in pieces; and if God did not wonderfully restrain their fierceness, the human race would be utterly destroyed" (Calvin 1965 [1554]: 290). In a modern context, where it is human action that threatens the existence of animal species rather than animals that threaten to kill large numbers of humans, it is unsurprising if our perspective and priorities are somewhat different. Indeed, Christian writers promoting a biblical vegetarianism deal with this passage by stressing that the permission to kill animals for food represents precisely a *permission* rather than a positive command, a permission which reflects the fact that human-animal relationships are not what they should be. It constitutes, in Andrew Linzey's words, "an accommodation to human sinfulness" (Linzey 1994: 127; cf. Webb 2001: 71). The ideal, which, it is argued, Christians should seek to practise now, is expressed in both the primaeval and eschatological visions, where plants provide all necessary food (Gen. 1:29–30; Isa. 11:6–9; see further ch. 8).

The second part of the speech concerns God's covenant, all too often referred to as "the covenant with Noah" (see, e.g., the headings given in NIV and NRSV). What commentators often fail sufficiently to note is the striking extent to which the covenant is emphatically and repeatedly said to be with all living creatures, indeed, with the whole earth (see vv. 10, 12, 13, 15, 16, 17; Olley 2000: 136). The opening declaration refers to the "covenant with you and your offspring after you, and with every living creature that is with you, the birds, the livestock, and every beast of the earth with you, as many as came out of the ark; it is for every beast of the earth" (Gen. 9.10, ESV). In concise form, it may be described simply as "the covenant between me and the earth" (9:13). The summary at the end refers to "the covenant that I have established between me and all flesh that is on the earth" (9:17, ESV). And it is explicitly an "everlasting covenant" (*berit 'olam*, v. 16, cf. v. 12).

Just as feminist writers have drawn attention to the unconscious androcentrism (male-centredness) that shapes the comments and concerns of biblical scholars, so too an awareness of ecological questions can serve to highlight the implicit anthropocentrism of commentators on this text. In a recent commentary on this passage, for example, John Hartley writes:

> God ... establishes a covenant with Noah and his offspring, guaranteeing never again to destroy the earth by a flood. This covenant gives humans confidence to build communities without fearing another catastrophe of total devastation ... The repetition of *every living creature* (... four times) and *all life* (... five times) stresses that God's covenant is with all humans. This covenant also concerns God's relationship to *the earth* ... which he mentions seven times. (Hartley 2000: 109–110, original emphases)

One of Hartley's concerns, it would seem, is to stress that the covenant is with *all* humanity and not just with a particular people or race. But his focus on humans does scant justice to the text's repeated emphasis on every living thing; this is emphatically a covenant which establishes God's promise and relationship to all creatures, to the earth community as a whole.

It is unsurprising, then, that ecotheologians have picked up on Gen. 9:1–17 as an especially relevant text. For Olley, for example, the covenant is a sign of "God's intention to keep together the rich biodiversity of the earth" (2000: 139). Steven Bouma-Prediger (2001) examines this passage under the heading "With whom does God make a covenant?" (p. 96), concluding that "God covenants with the earth and all its creatures. An everlasting covenant. An unconditional covenant. God covenants with us his faulted people and with this his groaning earth. The God who remembered Noah and all the animals in the ark also re-membered the earth" (p. 99). As such, this text offers an important contribution to an ecological reading of the biblical story, and a corrective to an overly anthropocentric focus.

Conclusion

These chapters of Genesis, then, offer some stimulating and significant material to an ecological biblical theology, especially in the depiction of God's covenant with all the earth in Gen. 9:8–17. Yet at the same time we must acknowledge that these chapters of Genesis do not unambiguously or straightforwardly resource an ecological theology and ethics. On the positive side, the text clearly implies an interconnectedness of humanity, animals and the earth. In both corruption and covenant humanity is inextricably bound up with the rest of the earth community. All the earth somehow slides into the degradation and corruption that begins with Adam and Eve's disobedience and suffers the curse-consequences. And all the earth is emphatically included in the covenant God makes after the Flood. But there is also a resolute and clear anthropocentrism, in both positive and negative senses. Negatively, it is humanity's wickedness that is central to the scene of corruption that God observes (6:5–6; 8:21). Positively, it is humanity which stands at the centre of the covenant made after the Flood – it is, after all, addressed in a speech to Noah and his sons. And it is humanity which is given a new and extended mandate not only to be fruitful and multiply but also to kill animals for food. As Olley rightly suggests, Genesis 9 offers "mixed blessings for animals". Moreover, there are many aspects of these texts that reflect their ancient context of production and assume mythological beliefs hard to accept in the modern world. What sense can we make of the corruption of animals and birds, or, more generally, of any notion of a "fall"? How far can we make sense now of a worldview in which divine creatures mate with human women, or in which animals are to be held accountable (by God) for acts of murder? There are important contributions to an ecological theology presented in these chapters of Genesis, but there are also ambiguities, ancient myths, and modes of anthropocentrism that make the appropriation of these contributions less than straightforward.

Further reading

Rogerson, John W., *Genesis 1–11* (OTG; Sheffield: Sheffield Academic Press, 1991).

Westermann, Claus, *Creation* (London: SPCK, 1974).

Fretheim, Terence E., *God and World in the Old Testament: A Relational Theology of Creation* (Nashville, TN: Abingdon, 2005), 69–89.

Wurst, Shirley, "'Beloved, Come Back to Me!' Ground's Theme Song in Genesis 3?" in Norman C. Habel and Shirley Wurst (eds), *The Earth Story in Genesis* (EB 2; Sheffield: Sheffield Academic Press, 2000), 87–104.

Olley, John W., "Mixed Blessings for Animals: The Contrasts of Genesis 9", in Norman C. Habel and Shirley Wurst (eds), *The Earth Story in Genesis* (EB 2; Sheffield: Sheffield Academic Press, 2000), 131–39.

Chapter 5

Creation's Praise and Humanity Decentred

Among the passages frequently noted in ecotheological writing are texts from the Psalms (especially Psalm 104) and Job (especially Job 38–40). There are good reasons for the focus on these texts, as we shall see. They are drawn from two different types of material in the Old Testament. The Psalms form a distinctive collection, probably deriving from the cultic worship of ancient Israel, especially in the Temple in Jerusalem. The various psalms date from a range of periods (both pre- and post-exilic) and are of various types, classically identified by Hermann Gunkel. Gunkel distinguished five major types: hymns (psalms of praise), communal laments, royal psalms, individual laments, and individual thanksgiving psalms (see Day 1990: 11–13). The book of Job belongs to the category identified by scholars as "wisdom literature", a group of books including, at their heart, Proverbs, Ecclesiastes and Job (see Hunter 2006: 3–25). These books, Alastair Hunter suggests, share a set of concerns: "(1) a universal perspective on life, (2) a humanistic view of the problems addressed, (3) evidence of curiosity about the natural and everyday world and (4) an intellectual approach to solving them [sic]" (p. 23). With our focus on ecological issues, there are two themes in these two bodies of literature that will particularly occupy our attention in this chapter: creation's praise and the de-centring of humanity.

Creation's praise in the Psalms

A number of psalms, especially those in the category of "hymns", focus on creation and its diverse wonders as a motivation for the worshippers to praise God. These are psalms of praise and thanksgiving. There are two main ways in which creation appears in these psalms, each of which deserves our consideration. The first is the appeal to creation as a manifestation of the greatness of God.

Creation as witness to God's greatness

There are a number of psalms which point the hearer to the greatness and wonder of creation as an indication of the greatness and praiseworthiness of God. A well-known example is the opening of Psalm 19: "The heavens declare the glory of God, and the sky above proclaims his handiwork" (Ps. 19:1, ESV). Here is an affirmation, Peter Craigie notes, "that the world of nature testifies, by its very existence, to God's glory" (Craigie 1983: 180). Similarly, Psalm 136 calls hearers to give thanks to God "for his steadfast love", listing a catalogue of wonders, including that God "by understanding made the heavens ... spread out the earth above the waters ... made the great lights ... the sun to rule over the day ... the moon and stars to rule over the night" (Ps. 136:5–9). Such a depiction of God as great creator is also found in Deutero-Isaiah, a prophetic book in which the focus on God as creator also comes to the fore (e.g., Isa. 40:12–31). The most extensive example in the Psalms is in Psalm 104, a lengthy hymn of praise and thanksgiving in which the reader/singer incites themselves to praise (cf. Psalm 103), that catalogues the works and wonders of God in creation. The content of the psalm displays parallels with an ancient Egyptian hymn to the sun, showing how the form and content of these Hebrew psalms reflects their wider cultural context (see Kraus 1989: 302; Allen 1983: 29–31). Also striking are the parallels with Genesis 1, particularly in the order in which the aspects of creation are mentioned, as set out in brief by John Day (1990: 41):

Ps. 104:1–4	Creation of heaven and earth	Cf. Gen. 1:1–5
Ps. 104:5–9	Waters pushed back	Cf. Gen. 1:6–10
Ps. 104:10–13	Waters put to beneficial use	Implicit in Gen. 1:6–10
Ps. 104:14–18	Creation of vegetation	Cf. Gen. 1:11–12
Ps. 104:19–23	Creation of luminaries	Cf. Gen. 1:14–18
Ps. 104:24–26	Creation of sea creatures	Cf. Gen. 1:20–22
Ps. 104:27–30	Creation of living creatures	Cf. Gen. 1:24–31

In this catalogue of the works of God in creation, "[t]he psalmist's concern ... is to portray Yahweh not only as creator but as sustainer of his world" (Allen 1983: 33). This focus on God's continuing activity is evident throughout much of the Psalm, for example in vv. 10–13:

> You make springs gush forth in the valleys; they flow between the hills; they give drink to every beast of the field; the wild donkeys quench their thirst. Beside them the birds of the heavens dwell; they sing among the branches. From your lofty abode you water the mountains; the earth is satisfied with the fruit of your work. (Ps. 104:10–13, ESV)

This celebration of all that God does to make and sustain the world is to some extent focused on its benefits for humanity (see vv. 14–15) but the Psalm, James Limburg claims, "is not human centered but all-of-life centered … In Psalm 104, humans are only a part of the great family of creatures the Lord has made" (Limburg 2000: 355). Certainly there is an emphasis on God's provision for all, animals and humans; all creatures depend on God for their food (vv. 21, 27). The Psalm as a whole paints a powerful and poetic picture of the dependence of everything on God. While humans are to look, to marvel, and to voice their praise, they are also to realize that they are part of this community of dependants. The perspective, we might say, is not anthropocentric, at least not strongly or primarily anthropocentric, nor even creation-centred, but theocentric – focused and centred on God, creator and sustainer of all things. As Hans-Joachim Kraus puts it, in his comments on this Psalm:

> The entire world is supported and controlled by deeds of God, toward which all elements and creatures are oriented … the entire creation is open to Yahweh; it is absolutely dependent on him, it dies without him. It lives on a creative act which is constantly effective in renewal … In this world the human being can react to the deeds and gifts of Yahweh only with daily praise that is conscious of its dependence. (Kraus 1989: 304)

This Psalm, and others like it, therefore invites ecological reflection, not only because of its portrait of the wonders of creation but also because of its setting of humanity firmly among the community of living things on earth. Two essays in the Earth Bible series take this reflection further, bringing Psalm 104 into dialogue with other traditional (and non-Western) views of the earth.

Arthur Walker-Jones sketches the Fijian notion of *vanua* (land) as a non-Western viewpoint from which to interpret this Psalm. In this world-view, in which the earth is regarded as a mother, "Earth has intrinsic worth because gods and ancestors are in *vanua* and gods, ancestors, people, flora and fauna are mutually interrelated and interdependent in their support of life" (Walker-Jones 2001: 86–87). Using this Fijian perspective to read the Psalm, Walker-Jones argues, enables the reader to avoid the traditional Western dualism that separates God from nature. Creation theology, he suggests, may be a problematic category, for it "has separated God from the Earth and we need … to ask whether these texts actually speak of God's presence in Earth" (p. 92, n. 11). Psalm 104 is important and illuminating, then, in various ways. In some ways it "reverses the curse of Gen. 3:14–19" (p. 91) – with its depiction of a renewed earth providing food and creating each new generation (pp. 91–92) – and it depicts humanity not as stewards or rulers of creation but as dependent *on* the earth: "Earth has no need of humans as partners and humanity has no special role as custodian" (p. 93). Moreover, according to Walker-Jones, in Psalm 104, "[h]umanity is part of a much larger landscape in which all parts have intrinsic value" (p. 94). The Psalm's picture of earth, he suggests, is comparable to James Lovelock's picture of earth as a living organism, and "modern ecology's understanding of the web of life" (p. 95). "The repetitions that tie Psalm 104 together, therefore, are suggestive of a diverse, interdependent and interconnected Earth community" (p. 95). A reading from a Fijian perspective, Walker-Jones proposes, shows Psalm 104 to reflect and support some of the ecojustice principles central to the Earth Bible project (see pp. 13–14 above).

Similarly, Abotchie Ntreh argues that "when Psalm 104 is read from a predominantly African perspective, the psalm reveals an impulse and a call for the survival of Earth" (Ntreh 2001: 98). "The psalmist, and indeed the African peoples, want us to realize that human life is intertwined with plant life, animal life and more. All parts of Earth – the entire Earth community – are mutually interdependent" (p. 102). Psalm 104 "calls us back to the wisdom of our forebears, to learn and apply their values towards Earth – both for its survival and our own … To save Earth and ourselves we need to return to the time-tested norms of African traditional religion and the values of Psalm 104, and marry them to the new scientific methods that are ecologically sound" (p. 108).

There is undoubtedly value in highlighting the depiction of earth, and of the relationships between God, earth and humanity, in the world-views of the psalmist and of contemporary indigenous peoples. These can challenge and offer alternatives to the modern Western world-views that underpin the consumer-focused (anthropocentric!) ideology central to contemporary capitalism. Yet there is also a danger in idealizing these alternative world-views, ancient and modern, as if all the problems stem (as Lynn White's thesis might imply) from the development of the Western industrial world-view. Ancient warfare, after all, included deliberate acts of destruction, such as are mandated in biblical injunctions (2 Kgs. 3:19, 25; cf. Deut. 13:15; Josh. 6:21; 1 Sam. 15:12–23). As Joseph Blenkinsopp reminds us:

> The environment was being devastated and species rendered extinct long before Judaism, Christianity, and their Scriptures appeared on the scene. The destruction of the Lebanon cedar forests was well under way by the second millennium B.C., and the Syrian elephant had been hunted to extinction by the seventh century B.C. If the Assyrians, mighty hunters before the Lord,

had been more technologically advanced, they would no doubt have done even more damage than they did to the flora and fauna of the Near East. (Blenkinsopp 2004: 36)

While Psalm 104's picture of an interconnected earth community dependent on God is of considerable importance, then, it cannot too easily be assumed to sustain, without further argument or articulation, an environmentally friendly worldview and associated practices.

Creation's praise of God.

Beyond the idea that the created cosmos reveals God's greatness and glory, a number of psalms present a call for the whole creation to join in praise of God. Again this is a motif strongly evident in Deutero-Isaiah (e.g., 44:23; 55:12) and occasionally elsewhere too (e.g., Joel 2:21–22; see Fretheim 2005: 267–68 for a list of Old Testament references, most of which are in the Psalms). For example, in Psalm 98 the call to praise goes out to all the earth:

> Make a joyful noise to the LORD, all the earth; break forth into joyous song and sing praises. Sing praises to the LORD with the lyre, with the lyre and the sound of melody. With trumpets and the sound of the horn make a joyful noise before the King, the LORD. Let the sea roar, and all that fills it; the world and those who live in it. Let the floods clap their hands; let the hills sing together for joy at the presence of the LORD, for he is coming to judge the earth. (Ps. 98:4–9, NRSV. Cf. also Pss 66:1–4; 96:1, 11–12; 97:1)

The most extended example of this depiction of creation's praise of God in the psalms is found in Psalm 148 (see further Fretheim 1987; 2005: 249–68). This psalm of praise, which begins and ends with the simple call "Praise the Lord!", falls into two main parts. "The first part of the psalm exhorts the heavenly world to the praise of Yahweh" (Kraus 1989: 562): "Praise the LORD from the heavens" (v. 1). We need to recall (see p. 24 above) that the Hebrew word for the heavens, *shamayim*, equally means the skies, and any modern distinction between spiritual or material realm can hardly be applied. The praise of the heavens includes angels and the divine host (v. 2), sun, moon and stars (v. 3), and "the waters above the heavens" (v. 4) – an indication of the ancient cosmology which saw waters above the sky and below the earth.

The second part of the psalm calls for praise "from the earth" (v. 7), from sea creatures, animals and birds, from the elements ("fire and hail, wind and frost"), from hills and trees, and from human beings too – though introduced in a "hierarchical order": kings, nations, princes and rulers (Kraus 1989: 563). Thus, "like a double choir, heaven and earth are situated over

against each other in Psalm 148. Both areas are called on to praise Yahweh"
(Kraus 1989: 564).

As Kraus and others indicate, aspects of the structure and content of
this psalm again reflect other ancient (Egyptian) traditions, which presented
encyclopaedic lists of the elements of nature (see Kraus 1989: 562; Allen
1983: 315). Here, though, the lists of the diverse aspects of the heavens and
the earth are brought together in a summons to praise Yahweh as the great
king of the earth, the most exalted one of all, who brings a means of salvation
to his people Israel (vv. 13–14). Similar material, perhaps derived from
Psalm 148, is found in what has become known as the *Benedicite*, part of
the Greek additions to the book of Daniel (see *The Prayer of Azariah* in the
NRSV Apocrypha; Brooke 2001: 708). Here, the three companions in the
fiery furnace join in a prayer of blessing to God, which includes an extended
call to all the elements of heaven and earth to join in blessing the Lord
(*Prayer of Azariah* 1:35–68).

The question, of course, is what to make of these depictions of all the
diverse facets of the cosmos being called to join in praise of God. Are they
metaphorical, or merely poetic imagery, a dramatic way of encouraging the
worshippers in Yahweh's temple to voice their praise? To some extent, to
be sure, the images have to be seen as metaphorical, and as
anthropomorphizing – constructing nature in human terms and images.
When the psalmist urges the floods to "clap their hands" and the hills to
"sing together for joy" (Ps. 98:8) we might quickly reply that floods have no
hands, and hills cannot literally sing. Yet we can also see how these
descriptions connect with, and interpret, the noises of the natural world.
It is, of course, a human decision, and one expressed in human language, to
describe the movements and sounds of the animate and inanimate world
as praise (compare the poem by Gerhard Frost quoted in Limburg [2000:
500], where a girl describes the crackling of a fire as clapping). This is a
theological interpretation of these phenomena. But is this an important or
valuable theological view of the created world?

Richard Bauckham has drawn attention to the theme of creation's praise,
arguing for its importance to an ecological spirituality (Bauckham 2002a:
176–77; 2002b). According to Bauckham, the implication of the biblical
material, primarily in the Psalms, is that

> [a]ll creatures, animate and inanimate, worship God. This is not, as modern
> biblical interpreters so readily suppose, merely a poetic fancy or some kind of
> primitive animism. The creation worships God just by being itself, as God
> made it, existing for God's glory. Only humans desist from worshiping God;
> other creatures, without having to think about it, worship God all the time.

There is no indication in the Bible of the notion that the other creatures need us to voice their praise for them. (Bauckham 2002a: 176–77)

Moreover, rejecting the idea that humanity fulfils a priestly role in mediating creation's praise to God, Bauckham suggests that "it is much more obvious that other creatures can help us to worship God than that we can help other creatures to do so" (Bauckham 2002b: 51). They do this "primarily by their otherness that draws us out of our self-absorption into a world that exists not for us but for God's glory" (p. 52). Indeed, a pressing need, with obvious ecological significance, is "to allow creation's praise by letting it be" (p. 52).

It needs to be noted, though, that none of the biblical texts, in the Psalms and elsewhere, quite says that creation actually worships God "just by being itself". Many, like Psalm 148, are a call or *invocation* to praise, with no more indication that non-human creation necessarily responds to the call, or already fulfils it, than that humanity does (Pss 69:34; 96:11–12; 98:7–8; 103:22; 150:6; Isa. 42:10–11; Joel 2:21–22). Some such texts also have a clearly eschatological context in view, a looking forward to the anticipated salvation of God in the future (Pss 96:11–12; 98:7–8; Isa. 42:10–11; Joel 2:21–22). Other texts, as we have seen, indicate that creation stands as testimony to God's glory and greatness (Pss 19:1–4; 104). Once again, then, the contribution of the biblical texts to an apparently valuable theological idea is less straightforward than may be supposed. Moreover, there are difficult questions about how we can make sense of this idea in a way which is compatible with our scientifically informed view of the world. What does it mean to say that a dog or cat praises God in its barking or miaowing? Or, still more difficult, perhaps, what it can mean to suggest that inanimate things lacking any form of consciousness we can discern – rocks and oceans, hills and trees – also express praise to God through their movements and noises? This is not by any means to imply that the motif of all creation's praise of God is not important, and a crucial biblical contribution to a contemporary ecological theology. But it does mean that the idea requires some creative interpretation and new thinking, when it is transplanted from the context of ancient Israel to the scientifically and ecologically aware context of the twenty-first century (see ch. 11 below).

The decentring of humanity in Job

In turning next to the book of Job, we turn to the category of wisdom literature. However, as we shall see, there are some evident links with the material we have seen in the Psalms, especially in Psalm 104. The wisdom literature has been somewhat less prominent in ecotheological discussion than the book of Genesis, due in considerable part to the heavy focus placed upon the crucial texts in Genesis 1 by the debate sparked by Lynn White (see chs 1 and 3 above). But a number of authors have sought to show its relevance to ecological concerns, suggesting that it may offer richer and more promising contributions. Katharine Dell, for example, relates the wisdom material to three concerns of modern "deep ecology": "interrelatedness and interaction"; "the well-being and flourishing of all human and non-human life in all its richness and diversity"; and the conviction that "the sustaining of life has inherent value and God is at the centre, creating and sustaining a process that is, in the final analysis, mysterious" (Dell 1994). Dell argues that "modern ecological principles can find some support in the wisdom literature", and that certain points of ethical guidance emerge from this biblical tradition: "there is a constant process of interaction at work", a process in which human beings have a responsibility to allow and foster its continuation; "nature has a value inherent in it. It exists for its own sake"; and "God is at the centre, creating and sustaining" (pp. 450–51). Ecotheologians such as Celia Deane-Drummond have also argued that the category of wisdom provides a particularly fruitful category with which to develop an ecological theology and ethics (e.g., Deane-Drummond 2000; 2004: 214–36). There are, of course, many texts in the wisdom tradition one might consider (see Johnston 1987; Dell 1994; Habel and Wurst 2001). But I shall focus on one example, already identified by a number of writers as of particular ecotheological interest: God's speeches at the end of the book of Job (Job 38:1–42:6).

The outline of the story of Job is well known: a righteous man is stripped of his possessions and family and given terrible sufferings to bear, as part of a test of his faithfulness to God. Three friends offer Job explanations for his suffering, none of which he can accept. Job maintains his innocence, confounding any theory which explains his suffering as a punishment or consequence of wrongdoing. Finally, near the end of the book, God appears on the scene, thundering two speeches at Job, whose response – a response which is very difficult to interpret (see Habel 1985: 575–83; Fretheim 2005: 232–33) – is apparently one of quiet resolution and acceptance of God's power (42:1–6). Perhaps the most persuasive view of these concluding exchanges is that Job has effectively levelled charges against God, insisting on his own innocence and demanding that God answer the case against him: that "God fails to govern the universe properly, that is, in such a manner that virtuous people thrive and wicked individuals come to grief", and that "at the very least God is guilty of criminal negligence" (Crenshaw 1992: 71). In Norman Habel's view, "Job's final speech is an appropriate two-pronged resolution of the conflict between Yahweh and Job which enables both parties to preserve their integrity" (1985: 578). Or, as Terence Fretheim sees it, Job is, in the end, "setting aside his case against God, withdrawing his words against God's governance of the creation and recognizing that what he had known about God and God's world was inadequate" (Fretheim 2005: 232–33). But how then do the speeches of God respond to the charges, and to the situation of Job's suffering?

Gerhard von Rad reports the view of many scholars, and no doubt many non-academic readers too, when he notes that "[a]ll commentators find the divine speech highly scandalous, in so far as it bypasses completely Job's particular concerns, and because in it Yahweh in no way condescends to self-interpretation" (quoted in Fretheim 2005: 234). In other words, in these speeches, God offers no explanation for Job's sufferings, nor for God's own action in allowing or causing such events. What we do find is a thundering voice "from the whirlwind" (Job 38:1) posing a series of questions to Job about his own knowledge, presence and power in creation. It is notable that these questions parallel some of the affirmations of God's actions listed as reasons to praise in Psalm 104:

Job 38:1–42:5 (NRSV)	*Psalm 104 (NRSV)*
Where were you when I laid the foundation of the earth? (38:4)	You set the earth on its foundations, so that it shall never be shaken. (104:5; cf. also Isa. 40:12, 21)
Or who shut in the sea with doors when it burst out from the womb? – when I made the clouds its garment, and thick darkness its swaddling band, and prescribed bounds for it, and set bars and doors, and said, "Thus far shall you come, and no farther, and here shall your proud waves be stopped"? (38:8–11)	You cover it with the deep as with a garment; the waters stood above the mountains ... You set a boundary that they may not pass, so that they might not again cover the earth. (104:6, 9)
Do you know when the mountain goats give birth? Do you observe the calving of the deer? Can you number the months that they fulfil, and do you know the time when they give birth? (39:1–2)	The high mountains are for the wild goats; the rocks are a refuge for the coneys. You have made the moon to mark the seasons; the sun knows its time for setting. (104:18–19)
Can you draw out Leviathan with a fishhook, or press down its tongue with a cord? (41:1)	There go the ships, and Leviathan that you formed to sport in it. These all look to you to give them their food in due season. (104:26–27)

In an extensive list of such questions, God appears to stress, over and over again, all the diverse aspects of the created world which Job does not understand, does not control, and has not witnessed. Moreover, these manifold facets of the world exist and are sustained by God without any reference to human presence, Job's or anyone else's. God makes rain fall "on a land where no one lives" (38:26), and provides land and food for the creatures (39:5–6). Job's response to the first speech (38:1–40:2) is to keep silence, refraining from pressing his case (40:3–5).

The second speech (40:6–41:34) contains a deeply ironic challenge to Job's power: "Have you an arm like God, and can you thunder with a voice like his? Deck yourself with majesty and dignity; clothe yourself with glory and splendour. Pour out the overflowings of your anger, and look on all who are proud, and abase them ... tread down the wicked where they stand" (40:9–12, NRSV). God describes the strength and ferocity of two great creatures – one of the land (Behemoth), one of the sea (Leviathan) – stressing that these are creatures made by God, yet beyond the control or mastery of anyone else, including Job and his fellow humans.

The cumulative impact of such poetic writing is considerable; but it offers no consolation or answer to Job's suffering. As James Crenshaw suggests, the speeches represent "the shattering of every human illusion of occupying a special place in God's sight" (1992: 70), and "an equally radical criticism of the anthropocentric presupposition of ancient sages. Human hybris bursts before this rapturous celebration of a universe in which women and men play no role other than that of awestruck witness to grandeur and terror" (p. 80). Furthermore, Crenshaw sees this not only as a demolition of human pride, but also as an indication that the problem of suffering remains a mystery, a problem that calls the whole "wisdom" enterprise into question: "In a sense, the poet has Yahweh announce the collapse of the sapiential enterprise, for the human intellect cannot guarantee wellbeing in the kind of world that Yahweh parades before a chastened Job" (p. 81).

Such observations on the divine speeches in Job should already indicate some of the reasons why ecological writers have found these chapters such an important and inspirational resource. Bill McKibben, for example, draws a parallel between the situation of Job and our contemporary environmental crisis:

> Job ... was struggling with the orthodoxy of his day – with the "obvious" notion that God dispensed prosperity to the good and punishment to the wicked. And we – late twentieth-century Westerners – are beginning to struggle with an orthodoxy of our own – the central economic and social idea that more is better, that growth is necessary. These two orthodoxies ... are

similar in that an examination of the facts (Job's innocence, our environmental predicament) calls them into serious question.

But they are similar in another way as well ... Both stem from the assumption that human beings are and should be at the center of everything. They are outgrowths of the human-centered or anthropocentric understanding that has dominated modern culture. (McKibben 1994: 33)

McKibben sees God's speeches in Job as a powerful description of "a world without people – a world that existed long before people, and that seems to have its own independent meaning" (p. 36). We are only part of creation, and need something like another Copernican revolution to realize that we are not at the centre (p. 37). The result: "[o]ur anthropocentric bias is swept away" (p. 42), replaced by two "imperatives from the voice in the whirlwind – the call to humility and the call to joy" (p. 63).

Similarly, in an essay in the Earth Bible series, Dale Patrick sees God's questions in the first speech (38:1–40:2) as "designed to put Job – and all humans – in their place" (Patrick 2001: 110). This discourse "envisages a created order independent of humans ... Nothing in this address speaks of the good of creation for humans ... Such a world has intrinsic worth apart from any human valuation" (p. 111). Indeed, Patrick continues:

nothing that God says indicates any particular preference for humans. The discourse "decenters" creation; it is decidedly not anthropocentric. This is a world designed for the benefit of the whole community of life, indeed of inanimate nature (by our definitions) as well. Humans must find their niche within this dynamic, dangerous, but vibrant ecosystem. (p. 113)

The point of the second speech (40:6–41:34), Patrick suggests, is that it is "warning humans to recognize limits on their power to dominate and to control their destiny ... If God decenters creation in the first address, God disillusions the human will-to-power in the second. In the Earth community humans are not created to dominate but to fit within the limits of their ecosystem" (pp. 114–15). God's speech from the whirlwind challenges the human project of seeking "to control nature through science and technology" and "invites us to take our place in a community of beings empowered by a creator who delights in the flourishing of life" (p. 115).

In a further essay on Job in the same volume of the Earth Bible series, Norman Habel develops a still more provocative argument. Reviewing the various interpretations of the hugely influential "dominion" text in Gen. 1:26–28 (see ch. 3 above), Habel proposes that the "Wisdom tradition in Job 38–39 challenges and apparently subverts the so-called royal dominion tradition ... represented in the Genesis text" (Habel 2001: 179). In Job 38, God's questions, which assume a negative answer, show that Job –

representing humanity as a whole – "does not possess the knowledge, skills or power to control creation" (p. 187). Job 39 then shows how incapable Job is of controlling the animals: the wild ox is unwilling to serve him (39:9), and the horse's might is terrifying (39:20). The depiction of the ox (39:9–12) may be seen as "a parody of the idea that humans should have dominion over wild beasts" (p. 188). In the description of the horse, Habel suggests, whether deliberate or accidental, the effect is "to reverse the perspective of Genesis 9", where humans evoke fear and dread from the animals (p. 188): even an animal humans might claim to have domesticated remains a terrifying creature. "Domestication as a form of domination is a sham" (p. 188). Thus, God's speech

> challenges Job – as a representative of primal humanity – to recognize that he cannot "rule" Earth or Earth community ... He does not have the knowledge to "care for" the mysterious world of the wild ... [and] does not have the power to control creation and command the dawn. And, ultimately, he does not have the option of dominating the living world around him. (p. 189)

Even if Job's descendants, as Fretheim notes, "have come a long way in furthering their understanding of creation" (2005: 243), the devastation we have caused and the problems (of our making) we cannot control, like global warming, make this challenge still powerful. Humans have readily assumed the mantle of rulers of creation, but have hardly shown themselves capable of exercising dominion over nature in an unequivocally benevolent and life-enhancing way. The radical challenge of Job is to dethrone and decentre humanity, to revise our vision of our place in the universe, and to construct a theology which is far less arrogantly anthropocentric. While Patrick speaks of the "decentring of creation", a more apposite phrase, in my view, would be the "decentring of humanity".

Conclusion

The texts and traditions we have considered in this chapter, then, offer powerful and provocative contributions to an ecological revisioning of Christian theology and ethics. The idea that creation not only stands as a witness to God's greatness and glory but also participates in the calling to praise and worship God implies a broader focus than is conveyed by the generally anthropocentric theological tradition, with its concentration on the *human* vocation (see ch. 11). The worshipping community, we might say, is a community which encompasses all things. The book of Job promotes this decentring of humanity from a different perspective, one in which

God provocatively challenges any human pretensions to special significance or possession of power. None of these ideas can simply be translated immediately or obviously into contemporary environmental principles; they reflect the ancient and mythological contexts of their production, and require some careful thought if they are to become meaningful to a scientifically informed and ecologically aware generation. But this kind of challenge – to cross the gulf separating ancient text and modern context – is implicit in all theological and ethical interpretation of the Bible. Perhaps more interesting is the question about which biblical images and texts might find a place at the centre of a reconstructed and ecological theology: as Habel suggests, there is a clear contrast between the perspective of Genesis 1 (and Psalm 8) and Job 38–41. One places humanity at the pinnacle of creation, endowed with a divine blessing to dominate the earth; the other punctures any sense of human superiority, and emphatically decentres humanity. It is clear enough that one image has been more influential than the other. But how might a biblically-shaped theology be reconfigured if the prioritization of images changed, and new lenses shaped our reading of the Bible?

Further reading

Day, John, *Psalms* (OTG; Sheffield: Sheffield Academic Press, 1990).

Eaton, John H., *Job* (OTG; Sheffield: JSOT Press, 1985)

Fretheim, Terence E. (1987), "Nature's Praise of God in the Psalms", *Ex Auditu* 3 (1987) 16–30.

——, *God and World in the Old Testament: A Relational Theology of Creation* (Nashville, TN: Abingdon, 2005), 249–68.

Habel, Norman C. and Wurst, Shirley (eds), *The Earth Story in Wisdom Traditions* (EB 3; Sheffield: Sheffield Academic Press, 2001).

Bauckham, Richard J., "Joining Creation's Praise of God", *Ecotheology* 7 (2002) 45–59.

McKibben, Bill (1994), *The Comforting Whirlwind: God, Job, and the Scale of Creation* (Grand Rapids, MI: Eerdmans).

Dell, Katharine J., "The Significance of the Wisdom Tradition in the Ecological Debate", in David G. Horrell, Cherryl Hunt, Christopher Southgate and Francesca Stavrakopoulou (eds), *Ecological Hermeneutics: Biblical, Historical, and Theological Perspectives* (London & New York: T.&T. Clark, forthcoming).

Chapter 6

JESUS AND THE EARTH: THE GOSPELS AND ECOLOGY

The writer to the Hebrews may have been convinced that Jesus Christ remains "the same, yesterday and today and forever" (Heb. 13:8), but new depictions of Jesus continue to emerge in each generation. These depictions are related to the particular agendas and issues of most concern to his interpreters. Jesus is claimed as a forerunner who anticipates and thus legitimizes a range of contemporary interests and commitments. For some, Jesus is a liberator, a kind of proto-socialist revolutionary who initiated a movement of radical social, economic and political transformation. For others, Jesus is a kind of proto-feminist, who proclaimed and enacted a message of equality which transcended social customs and gender distinctions. And so on. The figure of Jesus stands, of course, at the centre of Christian theology, so it is natural that Christian theologians and ethicists appeal first and foremost to Jesus when they want to argue for a certain model of Christian belief and behaviour.

When some contemporary Christian writers argue in favour of a commitment to vegetarianism – to take an example closer to the topic of ecology – it is therefore understandable that they consider the figure of Jesus, seeing in him some kind of precedent for an ethical vegetarianism. Jesus, it is noted, is not explicitly recorded as eating meat in the Gospels. The "possible exception" of the Passover is uncertain, Andrew Linzey suggests, since "it is not entirely clear that Jesus ate the traditional Passover meal" (Linzey 1994: 132). Linzey concedes, nonetheless, that Jesus ate fish (some writers go further, suggesting that an originally vegetarian Jesus has been falsely depicted as eating fish by the Church-based producers of the canonical Gospel accounts) and sees this as the issue needing a response (pp. 132, 134). The most convincing answer, Linzey suggests, is that "sometimes it can be justifiable to kill fish for food in situations of necessity … real necessity for human survival, such as may be argued in the case of Jesus himself" (pp. 134–35). Furthermore, Jesus is presented in the Gospels as "identifying himself with the world of animals" (p. 135). Similarly,

Stephen Webb finds enough evidence to call Jesus "a lover of animals" (Webb 2001: 137), who may be classed as "a 'loose' vegetarian" who "avoided meat whenever that was consistent with his ministry" but did not wish to draw "undue attention to that dietary choice" (pp. 134–35).

Recalling the categories I set out in Chapter 1, we may see such interpretations of Jesus as examples of readings of recovery. In other words, despite what may be depicted as a general "failure" to see Jesus in this way before, a new interpretation can, it is claimed, show that he offers support and precedent for a contemporary model of Christian commitment, whether that be liberationist, feminist, vegetarian, or whatever.

Jesus the proto-environmentalist

It is no surprise, then, that ecotheological writers have turned to the depictions of Jesus in the Gospels, finding in Jesus support for a model of concern for the environment and care for God's creation. Against the negative charge of Lynn White and others, that the Christian tradition has encouraged an aggressive human domination and exploitation of nature, such approaches seek to show that a more positive picture can be found in the Bible, and specifically in the Gospels. Sean McDonagh, for example, writes:

> A Christian theology of creation has much to learn from the attitude of respect which Jesus displayed towards the natural world. There is no support in the New Testament for a throw-away consumer society which destroys the natural world and produces mountains of non-biodegradable rubbish ... The disciples of Jesus are called upon to live lightly on the earth ... Jesus shows an intimacy and familiarity with a variety of God's creatures and the processes of nature. He is not driven by an urge to dominate and control the world of nature. Rather he displays an appreciative and contemplative attitude towards creation ... The gospels tell us that nature played an important role in Jesus' life. (McDonagh 1990: 158; cf. also McDonagh 1994: 140)

McDonagh continues, noting that Jesus spent "formative" time "in the desert", "regularly returned to the hills to pray" and "regularly interspersed" his teaching "with references to the lilies of the fields (Luke 12:27), the birds of the air (Matt 6:26), and the lair of foxes (Luke 9:58)" (pp. 158–59).

Other writers draw attention to some of the same material, citing Jesus' references to God's care for birds (Matt. 6:26; 10:29; Luke 12:6, 24) and flowers (Matt. 6:28) or noting the extent to which his parables employ imagery of the natural world and agriculture (e.g. Matt. 13; Mark 4:1–20, 26–32; John 15:1–8). These features of Jesus' teaching are seen as indicating his sense of God's care for the non-human creation and his own sensitivity towards it (e.g., Cooper 1990: 172, 218; Northcott 1996: 224–25; Hill 1998: 80–82).

As is the case elsewhere in the Bible, ecotheological engagement with the Gospels seems heavily focused on a few favourite or crucial texts. This is in part a reflection of the fact that there is little material of obvious or explicit ecological relevance in the Gospels: Jesus does not talk, at least not directly, about humanity's role in relation to creation or about any responsibilities we might have towards animals, plants, or the earth in general.

One attempt to move beyond the citation of the few obvious texts has been made by James Jones (2003), who draws attention to the various kinds of Gospel sayings describing Jesus' role as the Son of Man. Some such sayings also refer to the earth, such as Matt. 9:26: "the Son of Man has authority on earth" (for a list see Jones 2003: 8–9). This suggests, Jones proposes, "that the earth is the arena of the mission of Jesus", a sign of Jesus' (and God's) "commitment to the earth, present and future" (p. 20). Jones also draws attention, among other things, to the number of animals mentioned in the Gospels, suggesting, like McDonagh, that this shows how "Jesus lived a life that was connected to the environment, to the animals and to the land. That's why his thoughts are shot through with images of the earth and a variety of God's creatures" (p. 51). In short, the mission and message of Jesus are not about enabling human beings to escape from the earth to heaven, but about the bringing together of heaven and earth, as expressed in the petition from the Lord's prayer: "your will be done, on earth as it is in heaven" (Matt. 6:10). As Son of Man, Jesus "is central to the earthing of heaven and the heavening of earth" (p. 62).

Critical reactions: Making Jesus in our image?

Such presentations of Jesus – whether as liberator, proto-feminist, vegetarian or pro-environment – are generally depicted as attempts to read or reconstruct from the biblical sources what is there, what Jesus really was like. Jones, for example, insists that he is "determined to read out of the text and not into it" (p. 7). McDonagh's sketch cites many Gospel texts in illustrating how Jesus referred and related to nature. Yet it is not hard to see how the contemporary agenda and its pressing concerns have shaped the kind of questions interpreters are asking and the kind of answers they find.

It is a long time since Albert Schweitzer presented his devastating criticism of the lives of Jesus written before his rigorously "historical" quest, in which writers had made a Jesus in their own image, finding their own moral values anticipated and reflected in his teaching. As Schweitzer put it:

> each successive epoch of theology found its own thoughts in Jesus; that was, indeed, the only way in which it could make him live. But it was not only each epoch that found its reflection in Jesus; each individual created Jesus in accordance with his own character. There is no historical task which so reveals a man's true self as the writing of a Life of Jesus. (Schweitzer 2000 [1913]: 6)

It is no surprise, then, that McDonagh the environmentalist and theologian finds a Jesus who models a life which avoids waste and over-consumption and displays a contemplative love and concern for nature; no surprise that Webb the loose vegetarian finds a Jesus who is precisely the kind of vegetarian Webb sees as the best model for Christians. To what extent this is a problem, or something to be avoided, is an issue to which we shall return.

First, though, it is worth considering briefly how well the Gospel texts support the depiction of an earth-loving eco-Jesus. It is hard to see, for example, how McDonagh can fail to see the calming of the storm (Mark 4:35–41), not to mention walking on water (Mark 6:48–50), multiplying food (Mark 6:47–51), raising people from death (John 11:38–44), and so on, as instances which sit awkwardly with his claim that Jesus "is not driven by an urge to dominate and control the world of nature" (1990: 158). It is at least questionable whether the fate of the Gerasene swine (Mark 5:11–13; Luke 8:32–33) or the fig tree (Mark 11:12–14, 20–21; Matt. 21:18–20) demonstrate that "God's care for creation was *assumed* throughout Jesus's ministry", as Tim Cooper suggests (1990: 218); or whether again we can square these texts with McDonagh's Jesus, who displays "an appreciative and contemplative attitude towards creation" (1990: 158), or with Michael Northcott's claim that "Jesus is portrayed as one who lives in supreme harmony with the natural order" (1996: 224). The more general point, on which Jones and others build a lot, that Jesus fills his teaching with references to animals, plants, and the earth, does not necessarily mean that Jesus thereby conveys or promotes a care and respect for creation. The prominence of such images primarily reflects the fact that Jesus lived in a pre-industrial agrarian peasant society, such that pastoral and agricultural images were simply the context and content of everyday life. Just as our jokes and stories might make reference to pubs, aeroplanes and money-markets, so Jesus makes reference in his parables to sowing and reaping, vineyards and fields, birds and flowers. After all, he never draws any implication from all his nature imagery that his disciples should therefore treasure and preserve the flowers and birds which they see around them. And, despite Jones's claims, the earth is simply, and obviously, the arena where the Son of Man conducts his mission and exercises his authority. The fact that Jesus makes reference to the earth as the place where he has come does not necessarily imply any particular valuation of it.

There is, of course, the oft-cited reference to God's care precisely for birds and flowers, among the favourite eco-texts in the Gospels:

> Therefore I tell you, do not be anxious about your life, what you will eat or what you will drink, nor about your body, what you will put on. Is not life more than food, and the body more than clothing? Look at the birds of the air: they neither sow nor reap nor gather into barns, and yet your heavenly Father feeds them. Are you not of more value than they? And which of you by being anxious can add a single hour to his span of life? And why are you anxious about clothing? Consider the lilies of the field, how they grow: they neither toil nor spin, yet I tell you, even Solomon in all his glory was not arrayed like one of these. But if God so clothes the grass of the field, which today is alive and tomorrow is thrown into the oven, will he not much more clothe you, O you of little faith? (Matt. 6:25–30, ESV; cf. Luke 12:22–28)

This passage clearly does reflect a belief in the general providential care of God for the whole of creation: God feeds the birds and clothes the flowers. But the final verse makes clear that this is in the context of an argument from the lesser to the greater, the purpose of which is to stress the far greater value of human life. This is a highly anthropocentric text! After all, the fine flowers are quickly described as transient vegetation, here today and burnt tomorrow. Indeed, the focus in this text on God's care for human beings, a response to the issue of human anxiety, shows the real concern to be the hard-pressed disciples, those who have left home and family – and the basis for their livelihoods – to follow Jesus. These itinerant missionaries or "wandering charismatics", Gerd Theissen has argued, in an essay first published in German in 1973, were a crucial group within the earliest Christian movement. Indeed, Theissen offered a cutting antidote to anachronistic and romanticizing readings of texts such as Matt. 6:25–34. Discussing this text, Theissen writes:

> We should not read into this saying the mood of a Sunday afternoon stroll with the family. It has nothing to do with delight in birds and flowers and green fields. On the contrary: what this saying is talking about is the whole

rigor of the life led by the wandering charismatics, outlawed, without any home and without protection, people who made their way through the countryside without any possessions and without any work. (Theissen 1993: 39–40)

It would seem, then, that the apparently relevant sayings of Jesus can go only a little way, if any way at all, towards establishing a basis in Jesus' actions and teaching for a positive environmental theology and ethics. Some general sense of God's care for all of creation is perhaps as much as can be claimed to emerge.

Potential for an ecological reading of the Gospels

The citation of apparently relevant material in the Gospels, then, cannot get us very far in terms of providing a biblical basis for an ecological theology. The many references to rural imagery or to the earth itself do not, it turns out, represent an expression of commitment to care for the earth nor even of the intrinsic worth of all creation. The focus of Jesus' message, and of his actions and miracles, all seem to be undeniably anthropocentric: not only birds and flowers but pigs and fig-trees too are evidently of lesser value than people.

What if we try to work on a broader canvas, and consider some of the central features of Jesus' proclamation and action? While much remains contested in contemporary Gospels scholarship, a strong case can be made that two features are among those central to the mission and message of Jesus, probably the so-called "historical Jesus" (i.e., as critically reconstructed from the various Gospel accounts), and certainly Jesus as he is presented in the Synoptic Gospels. These features are, first, the announcement of the reign or kingdom of God (e.g. Mark 1:15; 4:11; 9:1), and second, the idea that Jesus saw the kingdom of God as breaking in through his own words and deeds; that is to say, that the kingdom of God is not entirely a future expectation, nor entirely realized in the present, but rather *inaugurated* in and through the ministry of Jesus. E. P. Sanders, for example, regards the first point as among the "certain or virtually certain" things to be said about the historical Jesus (Sanders 1985: 326). Sanders regards the second as "possible", but no more than this, despite the confident claims of many to the contrary (p. 140; see pp. 129–40). Gerd Theissen and Annette Merz, however, in a standard work on the historical Jesus, see good grounds for regarding both the future and the present statements about the kingdom as authentic (1998: 261; see pp. 240–80). They conclude:

> The kingdom of God is both present and future. The time of fulfilment is already here, and Satan has already been conquered. Sayings about fulfilment and struggle (the conflict between the realms of Satan and God) express a present eschatology. The sayings about the dawn of the kingdom also have a present sense; they indicate in paradoxical formulations and images that a new world is beginning in the midst of the old. But only the future will bring the full realization of the kingdom of God. (Theissen and Merz 1998: 275)

Whatever is the case with the historical Jesus, it seems clear that the evangelists – Mark probably least so – did hold some form of "inaugurated eschatology", with the still-expected kingdom present and visible, albeit partially and proleptically, in the ministry of Jesus and the lives of the Christian communities (see the discussion in Theissen and Merz 1998: 256–61). Crucial texts include the following:

> But if it is by the Spirit of God that I cast out demons, then the kingdom of God has come upon you. (Matt. 12:28/Luke 11:20, ESV)

> Being asked by the Pharisees when the kingdom of God would come, he answered them, "The kingdom of God is not coming with signs to be observed, nor will they say, 'Look, here it is!' or 'There!' for behold, the kingdom of God is in the midst of you". (Luke 17:21 ESV; cf. GosThom 3, 113)
> (See also Matt. 11:12–13/Luke 16:16; Matt. 11:2–6/Luke 7:18–23)

Theissen and Merz also argue that a sense of the kingdom's presence is indicated in Mark 1:15–16 (pp. 256–57), and that present and future perspectives are combined in the Lord's Prayer (pp. 261–64).

One crucial question regarding any possible contribution of the Jesus tradition to a Christian environmental ethic is of course whether the kingdom – and the future fulfilment which is anticipated – implies the end of the present, earthly creation. This is a question we shall consider in later chapters (see chs 8–9). For now, we may note that the idea of an inaugurated eschatology strongly suggests a sense of *continuity* between old and new, since the characteristics and changes that define the future kingdom are said to be already visible in the present.

In terms of what defines the characteristics of the reign of God, it is the prophetic visions of the Old Testament, especially of the book of Isaiah, that most obviously inform the depictions presented in the Synoptic Gospels (see further ch. 8). In a programmatic declaration, placed in Luke at the outset of Jesus' ministry, Jesus reads in the synagogue from the prophet Isaiah:

> "The Spirit of the Lord is upon me, because he has anointed me to proclaim good news to the poor. He has sent me to proclaim liberty to the captives and

recovering of sight to the blind, to set at liberty those who are oppressed, to proclaim the year of the Lord's favour." And he rolled up the scroll and gave it back to the attendant and sat down. And the eyes of all in the synagogue were fixed on him. And he began to say to them, "Today this Scripture has been fulfilled in your hearing". (Luke 4:18–20, ESV)

Although this particular report is unique to Luke's Gospel, the famous beatitudes, edited by Matthew and Luke from a shared source generally labelled Q, draw on a similar tradition in their declaration of blessing for the poor and oppressed (Matt. 5:3–4/Luke 6:20–21). And another Q tradition, common to Matthew and Luke, has Jesus quoting the same text from Isaiah (Isa. 61.1–2) when he replies to a question from disciples of John the Baptist concerning whether he is "the one to come": "Go and tell John what you hear and see: the blind receive their sight and the lame walk, lepers are cleansed and the deaf hear, and the dead are raised up, and the poor have good news preached to them" (Matt 11.5//Luke 7.22, ESV).

Adrian Leske's Earth Bible reading of Matt. 6:25–34, the favourite text we have already considered, sets the passage against the background of the prophetic depictions of the restoration and renewal of creation (Leske 2002). Thus, "Matthew ... demonstrates that Jesus has come to fulfil the message of Isaiah and the prophets by proclaiming the good news of the kingdom of God" (p. 21). The imagery of food, drink, and clothing, Leske suggests, all relate to the anticipated celebration of the kingdom of God, often pictured in terms of a banquet (p. 23). "The good news of the kingdom of God ... is that God's reign is here now as well as in the future" (p. 25). However, Leske is perhaps still rather over-optimistic in his reading of this passage when he argues that the (ecojustice) principles (see pp. 13–14 above) of interconnectedness and the mutual kinship of humans and all created things are implicitly promoted here (see pp. 15–17, 27). The fact that "[h]uman beings are to learn from other members of the Earth community how God takes care of his creation" (p. 17) does not necessarily imply any profound sense of interconnectedness; the birds and flowers simply serve as analogies from which the disciples may learn of the (much greater!) care of God for them. And the disciples' relationship to God as Father does not strongly convey the sense that this implies a "kinship with other members of Earth community" (p. 26), except in the rather minimal sense of presuming that God is the providential creator of all things.

Another attempt to interpret the Gospels against the background of the prophetic vision of creation's renewal is Richard Bauckham's reading of the short phrase in Mark 1:13: "he was with the wild animals" (Bauckham 1994). In this brief phrase Bauckham sees an allusion to the theme of eschatological harmony, and specifically the idea that the Messiah would (re)establish peace with and among all creatures. As we have seen (see ch. 4), Jewish tradition saw enmity between humans and animals, and predation in the animal world, as signs of the distorted relationship that followed from the corruption of "all flesh", that is, all living things. There were, Bauckham suggests, two ways in which it was thought possible to overcome this disruption: in the life of the righteous person, who would be at peace with the animals (cf. Job 5:22–23) and in the messianic age, when the Davidic Messiah would establish just such a peace (see esp. Isa. 11:1–9). So, Bauckham argues, "it is the messianic peace with wild animals that Jesus establishes ... Isa. 11:6–9, the classic vision of the messianic peace with wild animals, is connected with Isa. 11:1–5, the classic prophecy of the Davidic Messiah. The peace with wild animals belongs to this Messiah's "righteous reign" (p. 19; see further ch. 8 below).

Bauckham's rich and suggestive study, while based on just four Greek words in Mark's Gospel, shows one way in which the depiction of Jesus can be seen to have ecotheological relevance. It is important to stress that such relevance can only begin to be drawn out when the Gospels' depiction of the inbreaking reign of God is enriched and informed by drawing on a wider range of biblical and later Jewish texts. Insofar as the Gospels themselves present the eschatological vision, it is anthropocentrically focused. The elements of Isaiah's visions that find echoes in the Gospels, for example, are those promising liberation for downtrodden and suffering people (Isa. 61:1–3; cf. Matt. 5:3–4/Luke 6:20–21; Matt. 11:5/Luke 7:22; Luke 4:18–19) not those which depict creation as a whole redeemed from the violence of carnivorous and venomous instincts (Isa. 11:6–9; 65:25). Isaiah's reference to the "year of the Lord's favour" (61:2) may be an allusion to the Jubilee year (cf. Lev. 25:10–55), which has implications for the land and its rest and restoration as well as for human beings. But this passes without explicit mention in Jesus' use of the Isaianic imagery. As Ernest Lucas observes:

> This Old Testament background enables us to see that Jesus' announcement of the coming of the Kingdom of God has ecological implications, even if they are not made explicit in the Gospels. Jesus' healing miracles should not be seen in a purely human-centred perspective. They are signs of the coming renewal of the whole created order. Jesus' nature miracles have a special significance in this regard. When he stills the storm on the lake, the way he speaks and the words he uses suggest an act of exorcism. It is not only humans that are under the sway of evil, needing to be set free from bondage to Satan through healing and exorcism. The same is true of the non-human creation, and Jesus' work of liberation embraces both. (Lucas 1999: 94)

So the inaugurated eschatology of the Synoptic Gospels might provide a framework within which the eschatological visions of the Hebrew prophets and their later interpreters become a matter for present realization and ethical demand, as well as future expectation. It may be, perhaps, that the inaugurated eschatology provides a central framework within which other texts and ideas might contribute to an ecologically relevant theology and ethics. But this constructive possibility remains to be explored further (see ch. 11).

History and hermeneutics

Finally, we return briefly to a point raised above, when I cited Schweitzer's critique of the "lives of Jesus" that had effectively presented a Jesus made in the image of his interpreters. I suggested that a similar observation can be made about many of the portraits of Jesus in contemporary theological writing, not least in ecotheology. But does this matter? Is it inevitable that we will "make" Jesus in our image?

Since the time when Schweitzer was writing we have come to be much more suspicious of any claim to present an objective historical account of Jesus (or of any historical figure), since it is now widely acknowledged that any historical portrait is inevitably shaped by the context, commitments and presuppositions of the interpreter. Depictions of Jesus, like interpretations of any other biblical figure or text, are a product and a reflection of a particular kind of location: cultural, political, economic, geographical, historical, and so on. So, in one sense, we do unavoidably make Jesus in our own image, or at least make Jesus in ways shaped by our own priorities and assumptions. Often this is unconsciously done, by people aiming to be rigorously detached and historical. Often too, particular constructions of Jesus (and the Bible more generally) turn out to be reflections, at least in part, of broader political or cultural convictions, such as notions of racial superiority and legitimate conquest; there have been regrettable links between mission and colonialism. Readers from other contexts and cultures, sometimes from among the oppressed and colonized, have then begun to produce their own counter-constructions and counter-readings, which challenge the hegemony of established scholarship.

But does this mean, then, that we must simply expect and accept that just as vegetarians and feminists, along with capitalists and free-marketeers, construct a Jesus who fits their own convictions, so too ecologists will construct an eco-Jesus, and that this is an important aspect of their attempts to promote and justify their own viewpoint? There are, I think, two extremes to be avoided. One is the extreme which claims simply to be engaged in disinterested historical reconstruction, to be presenting a historical depiction of Jesus entirely uninfluenced by any contemporary agenda or commitment. Such detachment, I think, has been shown to be illusory. But the other extreme is one in which we simply accept that each interpreter, each interest group, will construct their own perspective or reading, and that each is, in a sense, a legitimate reflection of that specific reader's or reading community's convictions. The problem here is to ensure that we do not lose the sense that such readings can and should be subjected to critical examination and found more or less plausible, for only with some wider sense of communicable plausibility can we retain the possibility that we might be able to persuade one another to change our views, to act and believe differently. In other words, we should endeavour to construct a plausible portrait of Jesus, acknowledging all the time that the portrait will be shaped, and perhaps distorted, by the specific priorities and questions we bring.

In a sense this brings us back to an issue that runs throughout this book thus far: by illustrating the range of possible interpretations and the difficulties (as well as the possibilities) for an ecological reading of biblical texts, I hope to make it clear that an ecological theology and ethics cannot emerge simply from "listening" to the Bible's message (as *The Green Bible*'s editors suggest). We have seen in this chapter how the attempts to appeal to certain Gospel texts as indications that Jesus loved nature and cared for the earth turn out to be rather implausible, and more a reflection of the interpreter's values than of the Gospel material. Yet at the same time there is also potential for constructing an ecological theology using material in the Gospels, linking, say, the inaugurated eschatological vision with material elsewhere in the Prophets. The issue that remains is to show how and why we should engage in such a constructive mode of interpretation; and how to do so without simply pretending that the Bible says what we want it to say, or, put differently, without pretending that Jesus was really a good environmentalist ahead of his time.

Further reading

Marsh, Clive and Moyise, Steve, *Jesus and the Gospels* (2nd edn; London and New York: T. & T. Clark, 2006).
Theissen, Gerd and Annette Merz, *The Historical Jesus: A Comprehensive Guide* (London: SCM, 1998).
Jones, James, *Jesus and the Earth* (London: SPCK, 2003).

Habel, Norman C., and Balabanski, Vicky (eds), *The Earth Story in the New Testament* (EB 5; Sheffield: Sheffield Academic Press, 2002).

Bauckham, Richard J., "Jesus and the Wild Animals (Mark 1:13): A Christological Image for an Ecological Age", in Joel B. Green and Max Turner (eds), *Jesus of Nazareth: Lord and Christ. Essays on the Historical Jesus and New Testament Christology* (Grand Rapids/Carlisle: Eerdmans/Paternoster, 1994), 3–21.

Horrell, David G., "Biblical Vegetarianism? A Critical and Constructive Assessment", in Rachel Muers and David Grumett (eds), *Eating and Believing: Interdisciplinary Perspectives on Vegetarianism and Theology* (London and New York: T. & T. Clark, 2008), 44–59.

Chapter 7

Paul and the Redemption of the Cosmos

The apostle Paul's influence on Christian theology, especially Protestant theology, is immense. His letters, especially his letter to the Romans, have massively shaped Christian understanding of what the gospel is all about. For Martin Luther, of course, it was Paul's letters, especially Romans and Galatians, that provided the crucial insights into God's message of justification by faith, by grace and not works. Justification by faith then became the central doctrine in that Protestant tradition of theology.

But that view of the gospel is clearly focused on human beings, on the question as to how guilty, sinful people find forgiveness from a righteous God. These are the issues on which Paul seems to concentrate: the salvation of human beings and their hope for resurrection to new life after death. Unlike the Old Testament, with its frequent focus on how the people of Israel are to live in the Land, Paul, like the New Testament generally, is more concerned with the new life which God has made possible through Christ, and with the age to come in which God's redeemed people will live, delivered from the hostile powers of sin and death. Certainly such topics have been the main focus for interpreters of Paul. As Brendan Byrne comments:

> Since Augustine in the fifth century ... the issue of justification by faith has dominated the interpretation of Paul in the Western theological tradition. This ensured that interpreters of Paul were engaged in a virtually exclusive preoccupation with relations between human beings and God. What Paul thought or wrote about human relationship to the non-human created world scarcely entered the picture. (Byrne 2000: 194)

When we approach the Bible with issues of ecology and the environment in mind, the initial question, naturally, is whether this focus in the reading of Paul's letters is justified. Is Paul's theology as focused on the salvation of human beings as has generally been assumed? That Paul's main concern is indeed with humanity, and specifically with the converts in the churches to which he writes, can scarcely be doubted. He says nothing explicitly about any need to care for the whole of creation or to value and preserve non-human creatures. Yet, as we shall see, there is more to say.

There are two texts in the Pauline letters that are frequently cited by ecotheologians: Rom. 8:19–23 and Col. 1:15–20. These two texts, in their different ways, seem to offer a broader picture, and suggest that Paul might have some important ideas to contribute to an ecological theology. We shall examine each in turn, before concluding with some broader reflections on the ecological implications and potential of the Pauline literature.

The groaning and liberation of creation: Romans 8:19–23

Romans 8 is set in the context of the wider argument of Romans 1–11, where Paul sets out the good news that he proclaims among the Gentiles. Having first established that all humanity stands condemned and imprisoned under the power of sin, Paul then sets out the answer God has provided to this problem. God has presented Christ as a sacrifice which makes justification of the ungodly possible. Just as Adam brought sin and death to all people, so Christ brings justification and life (Rom. 5:12–21). Christ's death to sin and resurrection to new life are "events" in which believers participate: in baptism they too die to sin and begin a new life, a life which is empowered by the Spirit and which anticipates the future resurrection of the body, the completion of the process of salvation. It is in the context of his comments about life in the Spirit, and his depiction of the certain hope that lies ahead, despite present suffering, that Paul mentions the creation (*ktisis*):

> For I consider that the sufferings of this present time are not worth comparing with the glory that is to be revealed to us. For the creation waits with eager longing for the revealing of the sons of God. For the creation was subjected to futility, not willingly, but because of him who subjected it, in hope that the creation itself will be set free from its bondage to decay and obtain the freedom of the glory of the children of God. For we know that the whole creation has been groaning together in the pains of childbirth until now. And not only the creation, but we ourselves, who have the firstfruits of the Spirit, groan inwardly as we wait eagerly for adoption as sons, the redemption of our bodies. For in this hope we were saved. Now hope that is seen is not hope. For who hopes for what he sees? But if we hope for what we do not see, we wait for it with patience. (Rom 8:18–25, ESV)

Most commentators agree that when Paul refers to *ktisis* here, he is indeed referring to "creation", that is, to non-human things, including non-human creatures, and not to a more specific creature or creatures, human or angelic (for this and the following points, see the discussion of Rom. 8:19–23 in Hunt *et al.* 2008). Somewhat more puzzling are Paul's references to creation as in "bondage to decay" and having been "subjected to futility". These enigmatic phrases are generally understood as allusions to the Genesis story, specifically the cursing of the ground following Adam's disobedience (Gen. 3:17). Paul clearly sees death as having "entered" the world as the consequence of Adam's sin, and as having spread to affect all – the whole created order, perhaps. This spread of death and corruption, then, is probably what is meant by the bondage to decay.

The subjection to futility (*mataiotēs*) is also difficult to interpret. Most commentators agree that it was God whom Paul intends to depict as the one who subjected creation, against its will, to this futility, perhaps as a consequence of the decay and death that had come to infect it. Just as in Rom. 1:18–32 humanity's refusal to know and worship God leads to God's "giving them over" to sinful passions, so, here, creation's (unwilling) bondage to decay leads to God's subjection of creation to futility, an inability to fulfil its true purpose or to escape the cycle of death and decay. While Paul does not explain in any detail what he means by his references to these past events of creation's bondage and subjection, he does indicate that they occurred, under God's control, in *hope* – a key theme in this chapter of Romans. Just as the suffering Christians at Rome hope for their final redemption, so the creation was subjected in hope, anticipating its final deliverance. Paul strikingly depicts the whole creation as groaning, as if in labour, as it anticipates its liberation from this bondage to decay. In particular, creation is straining to see the "sons/children of God" revealed, since it is the freedom of the glory of these children – most likely a reference to Christian believers – which creation longs and hopes to share.

The idea that the arrival of the age to come would be preceded and accompanied by tribulations which might be compared to labour pains is already familiar from Jewish literature before and around the time of Paul (Isa. 13:8–13; 66:5–16; 4 Ezra 10:6–16; cf. Mark 13:8). As James Dunn comments:

> the reversal of Adam's fall naturally requires the reversal of the curse on the ground (Gen. 3:17–18 ...); and the conviction that the whole created order would be caught in the tribulations introducing the age to come was already a firm part of the end-time scenario which Paul here draws on ... Paul's thought is clearly that creation itself must be redeemed in order that redeemed man may have a fitting environment. (Dunn 1988: 469–70)

Paul clearly parallels Adam and Christ, regarding them both as figures whose actions have affected the whole of humanity, indeed, it seems, the whole of creation (Rom. 5:12–21; 1 Cor. 15:22). If the impact of Adam's sin was universal, bringing decay and death throughout creation, then, so Paul's logic seems to run, God's work of redemption, restoring what was lost, can and must encompass the whole created order, or else it remains only a very partial reversal of the earlier pattern of decay and death.

Ecological interpretation of Romans 8:19–23

What, then, are the ecological implications of this text? How might it be useful, if at all, for ecotheology? As I have already mentioned, this text has been among the most frequently cited (though often only with brief discussion) in ecotheological writing. This is because it is seen as an important support for the idea that God's saving purposes do not include only human beings, but the whole creation. The description of creation as "groaning" is often taken up as an apposite depiction of the degradation of the natural environment (e.g. Bouma-Prediger 2001: 40), coupled with the hope for "cosmic redemption" (McDonagh 1990: 163). Thus, the Evangelical Declaration on the Care of Creation announces "full good news for all creation which is still waiting 'with eager longing for the revealing of the children of God'" (in Berry 2000: 19).

In an essay in the first volume of the Earth Bible series, Brendan Byrne (2000) sets out an ecological reading of this passage. An important part of the background of this text, and specifically of Paul's reference to the groaning of creation, according to Byrne, is the principle of a "common fate" shared by humanity and creation. Paul takes from Gen. 1:26–28 a "basically 'triangular' pattern ... where human beings play a leading and indeed determining role in creation" (p. 198). But the shared fate of humanity and creation can be for good or ill, depending on whether the fate is that of what Byrne calls the "sin story" represented by Adam or the "grace story" represented by Christ (pp. 198–200). The sin story, in which Adam subdues the earth – Byrne's minority reading of the subduer in Rom. 8:20, which most commentators take to refer to God – can allow us "to view human maltreatment of the material world as part of ... the 'sin story' of the human race" (p. 199). By contrast, the grace story suggests what is possible when human beings, in and through Christ, begin a "grace-filled, rather than a sin-driven, human role in the universe ... Human partnership and custodianship of the material world is then a genuine enactment of the grace of God, operative in Christ" (p. 200). Paul's depiction is, then, unavoidably anthropocentric, though not in a negative way (p. 198). In a more recent treatment, Byrne suggests that as

> human action impinges upon the world for good (as a response to grace) and for ill (as a manifestation of captivity to sin), then we can acknowledge that, in Pauline terms, the future of the world (salvation) does to some extent lie in human hands. It is not *simply* God's gift and it remains ours to lose. Hope for the future in this sense takes human action into account. It remains hope in God but it is also hope in the prevailing power of God's grace *working through*, not around or above human cooperation. (Byrne forthcoming)

Robert Jewett (2004) sets Romans 8 against the background of Roman imperial ideology, which depicted Augustus as inaugurating a glorious new age of peace and flourishing, with images of fertility and fecundity in the natural world. Paul, by contrast, insists that the present age is still one of suffering and groaning and that the "sons of God", not Caesar, are the ones through whom creation's restoration will be brought about:

> In a vision with extraordinary relevance for the modern world, Paul implies that the entire creation waits with bated breath for the emergence and empowerment of those who will take responsibility for its restoration, small groups of the *huioi tou theou* (sons of God) ... These converts take the place of Caesar in the imperial propaganda about the golden age, but they employ no weapons to vanquish foes ... As the children of God are redeemed by the gospel, they begin to regain a rightful dominion over the created world (Gen. 1:28–30; Ps. 8:5–8); in more modern terms, their altered lifestyle and revised ethics begin to restore the ecological system that had been thrown out of balance by wrongdoing (Rom. 1:18–32) and sin (Rom. 5–7). (Jewett 2004: 35)

Recalling our earlier discussion of Genesis 1 (see ch. 3), it is notable that Jewett sees human dominion – properly understood and enacted – as central to this ecological vision. Like Byrne, Jewett sees Paul's text as essentially anthropocentric, since the children of God are central to the story of creation's restoration.

Reasons to be cautious: Is Romans 8 so eco-friendly?

Despite its status as one of the favourite texts for those seeking biblical support for environmental care, there are reasons at least to be cautious about the extent to which Rom. 8:19–23 can supply the basis for an ecological theology and ethics.

For a start, it is clear, as elsewhere in Paul, that the outlook here is fundamentally theocentric, that is, focused on God. The implied agent of the passive verbs which describe creation's past and future – "was subjected", "will be liberated" – is God. That raises two issues: first, the decision to subject creation to futility was God's, for whatever reason, so that God bears primary responsibility for the state of groaning in which the world currently finds itself. Second, the liberation which is hoped for is also something to be brought about by the action of God. Paul does not say here, at least not explicitly, that humans have a role to play in helping to "liberate" the creation. The main thrust of the text is to encourage a suffering, vulnerable minority group to endure their suffering, with a sure hope that God will bring final deliverance. Romans 8 does not, then, *directly* supply an ethical imperative for Christians "to work toward the goal of creation's final transformation", or even "to be involved in working toward those ends that God will finally secure through his own sovereign intervention" (Moo 2006: 474, 484).

A second key issue is that the passage is undeniably anthropocentric: what creation longs to see is the revealing of the sons of God (v. 19) and what it longs to share is the freedom of the glory of the children of God (v. 21). Moreover, the whole passage belongs within a literary context the focus of which is the redemption of humanity, Jew and Gentile alike. For some ecotheological writers, such anthropocentrism is a problem, and requires criticism and rejection; essays in the Earth Bible series, for example, often embody this criticism of perceived anthropocentrism in the biblical texts. The ecojustice principles which shape the Earth Bible Team's approach emphasize instead the intrinsic worth of "the universe, Earth and all its components" and the notion of "mutual custodianship": "Earth is a balanced and diverse domain where responsible custodians can function as partners, rather than rulers, to sustain a balanced and diverse Earth community" (see above, pp. 13–14). It would seem difficult to claim Romans 8 as a source for a radically non-anthropocentric theology; whether this should be an aim or not is an issue to which we shall return (see ch. 11).

Finally, Romans 8 is a profoundly eschatological text. That is, it is thoroughly infused with the idea that the present is a time of yearning, groaning, looking forward, to a day when the process of salvation will be completed and the suffering Christians of Rome, together with all creation, will be free from all that currently oppresses and harms them, free from death and decay. While this may certainly form a positive and inspiring vision, this future state, quite apart from the fact that it will be God's achievement, not a human accomplishment (see above), lies utterly beyond the present world, in which suffering and death are inevitable. Such a "new creation" is so radically different from the world we currently inhabit that it is difficult to see how being eco-friendly – reducing our carbon footprint, recycling our rubbish, and so on – can be seen as contributing to its arrival. Furthermore, if God, and only God, can and will redeem humanity and liberate creation, then what need is there for our marginal efforts to improve it here and now?

As we will see in Part III of this book, such sceptical questions are not intended to deny that texts such as Romans 8 can and do have an important contribution to make to an ecological theology rooted in the Bible. What I do intend to show, however, is that such texts do not, by themselves, straightforwardly or unambiguously provide a blueprint for ecological theology or environmental ethics.

All things reconciled in Christ: Colossians 1.15-20

The other Pauline text very often cited as offering biblical support for ecotheology is Col. 1:15–20. Colossians itself is among the letters whose authorship is disputed, with scholars disagreeing as to whether the letter was most likely written by Paul himself or by a co-worker or later follower of Paul's. Questions of authorship become even more complicated, however, due to the frequent identification of this particular passage as an early Christian poem or hymn, which may have been composed prior to the writing of Colossians, and by a different author (see Gordley 2007: 3–16). The text does indeed seem to have at least a poetic, rhythmic style and many scholars have divided it into two main sections, set out here side by side to show their parallel structure and content:

He is the image of the invisible God,	And he is the head of the body, the church.
	He is the beginning,
the firstborn of all creation.	the firstborn from the dead,
	that in everything he might be pre-eminent.
For by him all things were created, in heaven and on earth,	For in him all the fullness of God was pleased to dwell,
visible and invisible,	
whether thrones or dominions	
or rulers or authorities –	and through him to reconcile to himself
all things were created through him and	all things, whether on earth or in heaven,
for him.	making peace by the blood of his cross.
And he is before all things,	
and in him all things hold together.	(Col. 1:15–20, ESV)

Some scholars conclude that a previously existing poem has been edited by the author of Colossians, perhaps to reshape and reorientate its ideas, applying them more specifically to the Church. It has been noted, for example, that the two phrases "the church" (v. 18) and "by the blood of his cross" (v. 20) are the only phrases in the hymn that are explicitly Christian in content. Moreover, it can be argued that these two phrases extend the length of lines of the poem in a way which makes them look like later additions. In this way, the author of Colossians may have edited the hymn to make it somewhat less cosmic than it might previously have been: the phrase "he is head of the body" may have referred originally to the whole cosmos as the body of Christ, influenced perhaps by the Stoic notion of the universe as a body infused by divine *pneuma* or spirit (see also Col. 2:19; van Kooten 2003). But the author of Colossians specifies that the body is the Church.

Others, however, have insisted that such reconstructions of earlier forms of the hymn are inevitably speculative, and that there is nothing to prevent our viewing it as a literary unity composed by one author, perhaps the author of Colossians (Stettler 2000). N. T. Wright, for example, argues that the exegete's first task "is to deal with the text that we possess" and to interpret the text within the context of the letter (Wright 1991: 100).

Scholars have also debated the influences on the author of the hymn. While some argue that the Jewish scriptures and traditions of interpretation can entirely account for the relevant influences (Stettler 2000), others stress the parallels with Greco-Roman philosophy, specifically Middle Platonism and Stoicism (van Kooten 2003). Still others reckon with influences from both these streams of tradition (Gordley 2007).

There are many significant aspects of this passage, which has been much discussed in the history of interpretation (see Barclay 1997: 56–68). It has been especially influential, of course, in the development of christological doctrine, given its lofty depictions of Christ as the image of God, the firstborn of all creation, the one in whom the fullness (of deity) dwells, and so on. But most relevant for ecotheologians are the depictions of Christ as the one in, through, and for whom all things were created, the one in whom all things hold together, and the one through and to whom God has reconciled all things (*ta panta*). It is widely agreed that *ta panta* does indeed refer to all created things; thus, like Rom. 8:19–23, though in a quite different way, this passage too indicates that the whole creation is bound up in God's redeeming purposes.

Christ is depicted not only as the one through whom (and for whom) creation took place, but also as the one through whom (and to whom) all things have been reconciled. In other words, the text not only looks back to Christ's role in creation at the beginning (cf. Gen. 1:1; John 1:1–3) but also depicts Christ's saving work on the cross as affecting the whole creation, bringing about its reconciliation and peace. In the Colossian hymn this reconciliation is depicted as having already been achieved (v. 20), though it is clear from elsewhere in the letter that the author also recognizes that there remains a future dimension to this process, and looks forward to the day when God's saving work will truly be complete (e.g., Col. 3:1–3; see Still 2004).

Reconciliation and the act of making peace seem to imply that something was previously awry, that enmity and division needed to be overcome. (Romans 8, we recall, referred to the bondage to decay and futility of creation as the problems needing a solution.) The hymn itself does not give any indication as to why there was this need for reconciliation. But references to rulers and authorities, things in heaven and on earth (vv. 16, 20; cf. 2:15), as well as references elsewhere in the letter to the cosmic spirits and powers (cf. 2:8, 20) suggest that at least part of the picture may be the need to bring rebellious powers, spiritual as well as human, into submission to the lordship of Christ (cf. 1 Cor. 15:25–28; Eph. 1:20–22; 6:12). Also implied in the hymn, so Christian Stettler argues (2000: 326–33), is the idea of new creation. This new creation, referred to elsewhere in Paul (2 Cor. 5:17; Gal. 6:15), is not merely the restoration of the original creation. Rather, as Stettler puts it, "the bringing into being of the whole creation for the Messiah (v. 16) first comes to fulfilment in the reconciliation of all things to Jesus (v. 20)" (p. 345, my trans).

Ecological interpretation of Colossians 1:15–20

As with Romans 8, though using different imagery, Colossians 1 is important for ecotheologians in depicting the whole of creation – "all things", *ta panta* – as reconciled to God in Christ. Joseph Sittler, in a famous 1961 address to the World Council of Churches, was the first to suggest this ecological significance to the cosmic Christology presented in Colossians: "the sweep of God's restorative action in Christ is no smaller than the six-times repeated *ta panta* ... and all things are permeable to his cosmic redemption because all things subsist in him" (Sittler 2000b [1962]: 39). Seeing the magnitude of the threat to nature, Sittler argued that it was time to explore the untapped potential in this cosmic Christology, a potential that could lead from doctrine to ethical engagement: "The way forward is from Christology expanded to its cosmic dimensions, made passionate by the pathos of this threatened earth, and made ethical by the love and the wrath of God" (p. 48).

In his much more recent commentary on Colossians, James Dunn comments on the universal scope of the Colossian hymn as follows:

> The vision is vast. The claim is mind-blowing. It says much for the faith of these first Christians that they should see in Christ's death and resurrection quite literally the key to resolving the disharmonies of nature and the inhumanities of humankind ... In some ways still more striking is the implied vision of the church as the focus and means toward this cosmic reconciliation – the community in which reconciliation has already taken place (or begun to take place) and whose responsibility is to live out ... as well as to proclaim its secret. (Dunn 1996: 104)

While Dunn does not explicitly link this affirmation with any point of modern ecological relevance, Steven Bouma-Prediger quotes Dunn's comment, seeing in Col. 1:15–20 an important depiction of the universal scope of God's reconciling work in Christ (Bouma-Prediger 2001: 108; see pp. 105–10). This, for Bouma-Prediger, forms part of the biblical story on which an ecotheology can be based.

Vicky Balabanski likewise sees the passage as one which offers an constructive biblical contribution to ecotheology (Balabanski 2008; forthcoming). She suggests that the essentially Stoic ideas on which the author draws present a cosmology in which the divine permeates all of nature, a "permeation cosmology" (Balabanski 2008: 157). This cosmology can help us to move "beyond anthropocentrism", since the passage includes *ta panta*, "the whole biosphere", in the scope of God's reconciliation (p. 158). Thus, for Christians, "the peace-making through Jesus' blood on the cross is a dynamic process ... It enables us to move towards a bio-centric cosmology, learning and relearning respect for the impulse towards life in all creation" (p. 159).

Cautionary comments on Colossians

Once again, though, we must pause to consider how far this text really gets us in terms of its contribution to an ecological theology and ethics. Despite its frequent citation in works of ecotheology, as if mere mention of the universal scope of reconciliation in Christ were enough to imply ecological commitments and implications, the text does not so straightforwardly connect with contemporary ethical concerns.

First, we need to note that the author of Colossians makes it clear that the body of Christ refers primarily to the Church (1:18). It is possible, as some interpreters have argued (see above), that this is an editorial addition by the author of Colossians to an earlier hymn or poem which may have implied that the body of Christ was the whole universe. Whether or not this is the case – and it is, in the end, impossible to be certain – the form of the poem as it is presented in our text has this particular ecclesial interpretation of the body of Christ. Moreover, as Balabanski notes, there is a question about the extent to which the focus on Christ implies a necessarily anthropocentric theology: "Just as feminist scholarship has posed the question of whether a male savior can save women, we ask whether a human savior can be salvific for other species as well" (Balabanski 2008: 153).

Second, the primary focus for the author's notion of the reconciliation God has achieved in Christ is the "powers and authorities", spiritual as well as earthly, angelic as well as human, as 1:16 makes clear (cf. 2:15). Since reconciliation was generally conceived as involving relations between personal beings, this is no surprise. The implications of the emphatic use of *ta panta*, "all things", together with references elsewhere to the "elements of the cosmos" (if that is the meaning of the enigmatic Greek phrase *ta stoicheia tou kosmou*: 2:8, 20), can certainly support the idea that the author does envisage and depict here a fully universal process, the reconciliation and incorporation of everything into Christ. Nonetheless, the references to powers and authorities should serve to remind us that the author's cosmology and world view are very different from those of many modern Westerners, and certainly by no means straightforwardly identifiable with ecological concern for the (material) planet earth. While we might be inclined to conceive of reconciliation as involving the establishment of harmonious and sustainable relationships between humanity and nature, the author of Colossians is more likely to have been thinking about rebellious angels and demonic powers being brought into subjection to Christ.

Finally, even if the author does depict a divine achievement which is truly universal and cosmic in its scope – the reconciliation of all things in Christ – there are no ecologically-related ethical implications explicitly drawn from this. As in Romans 8, this work of cosmic reconciliation is the work of God, not of humans, and the ethical instructions that do feature in the letter to the Colossians concern the relationships of Christians with one another (3:8–17) or in the household context (3:18–4.1). It would of course be anachronistic to expect the author of an ancient letter to see ecological dimensions and ethical implications deriving from a passage such as the Colossian hymn. But this only serves to underscore the point that we cannot find ecotheology and ethics directly in the biblical texts. Our task will require something more than careful exegesis.

Beyond the favourite texts: Potential for an ecological reading of Paul?

While Romans 8 and Colossians 1 offer significant contributions to an ecological biblical theology, it is important, as with the Gospels (see ch. 6), to consider whether other texts and themes in the Pauline letters might also offer fruitful material. Again, this will mean moving beyond the most obviously relevant texts and beyond the meaning and concerns directly apparent in the texts.

For example, while debates over what constitutes the heart of Paul's gospel continue (justification by faith? participation in Christ?), it may be valuable, from an ecological perspective, to focus on the theme of *reconciliation*, a theme we have already seen in Colossians 1. In a theologically rich text in 2 Cor. 5:14–21 Paul speaks of "new creation" in Christ (v. 17), and sums up the Christian gospel in the following way: "in Christ God was reconciling the world to himself" (v. 19). It seems likely that what *Paul* had primarily in view here was the "world" of human beings, but given the way in which other texts in Paul invite a broader conception of the process of salvation, we may at least reasonably take this to depict a wider act of reconciliation, in which "all things" (to echo Colossians) are bound up (see Horrell forthcoming a). Paul evidently sees as a central achievement of the Christian gospel the overcoming of distinctions and divisions, and the creation of unity – all aspects of a process of reconciliation. In this too his own focus is on the overcoming of distinctions between *human* groups, as in the famous declaration of Gal. 3:28: "There is no longer Jew or Greek, there is no longer slave or free, there is no longer male and female; for all of you are one in Christ Jesus" (NRSV). But, in a context very different from that which Paul inhabited, and with different concerns and priorities, we might perhaps develop this to encompass non-human as well as human creation. Of course, as with other texts and themes we have studied, the idea of universal reconciliation does not easily or straightforwardly translate into any environmental ethical policies. But it does perhaps suggest a certain shape and focus for an ecological theology. Moreover, as with the Synoptic Gospels, Paul's eschatology has an inaugurated character: the new creation which God is bringing about in Christ is, in a sense, already here, but also not yet here. This implies that the characteristics of that new creation – most obviously those of peace and reconciliation – should shape and inform Christian action now in anticipation of its future fulfilment, even if that final fulfilment implies a world beyond the realm of our present experience (see ch. 11 below). Indeed, Paul's ethics have generally been understood as intimately connected with his theology, based on the conviction that Christians should "be what they are" in Christ, that is, should live in a way which reflects their identity as people who have died to their old life and now live anew in the power of the Spirit, part of God's new creation (2 Cor. 5:17; Gal. 6:15).

Paul's ethics, like his theology, are primarily and obviously focused on inter-human relationships, and specifically on the relationships among the members of the churches to which he writes. But again there may be the potential to take some the central principles of Pauline ethics, and extend and apply them to broader environmental concerns (see Hunt 2009). For example, arguably one of the most fundamental meta-moral principles in Pauline ethics is that of "other-regard", modelled on the self-giving of Christ for others. Christians are urged to look to the interests and concerns of others (see Horrell 2005: 166–245; Rom 15:1–3; 1 Cor. 10:24; Phil. 2:4–11). If the message of Paul's gospel is that the self-giving death of Christ makes possible the reconciliation and final liberation of the whole creation, then a logical corollary of this is that the scope of Christian other-regard should extend to the whole creation too. Again, what this would or should mean in specific concrete situations is far from obvious, but it does indicate one way in which the Pauline material might give a certain shape to a biblically-informed environmental ethics.

Conclusion

It is clear why ecotheologians have found Rom. 8:19–23 and Col. 1:15–20 to be important and obvious texts to appeal to in Paul's letters. They are among the few texts in the Pauline corpus where the scope of interest explicitly widens beyond the redemption of humanity. In their different ways, both texts indicate that God's saving purposes do encompass the whole of creation. Creation is not merely the stage on which the drama of human salvation takes place. These texts thus support two of the ecojustice principles: the intrinsic worth and the purpose of the earth (see above, pp. 13–14). However, it should also be clear that mere citation of these texts does not get us very far. Their ancient cosmologies and their theological and eschatological focus do not immediately support the environmental agenda, nor do these texts offer any explicit indication that ecologically relevant ethical implications might follow from them. This is not to imply, as the final section of this book will make clear, that they are unimportant or of little value in attempts to use the Bible to generate an environmental theology and ethics. But what it does imply, once again, is that we cannot simply read such theology and ethics direct from the pages of the Bible. As the final section of this chapter has hinted, a more constructive and creative mode of biblical interpretation will be required in order to engage these and other Pauline texts in shaping responses to the contemporary issues of ecology and the environment.

Further reading

Horrell, David G., *An Introduction to the Study of Paul* (2nd edn; London and New York: T. & T. Clark, 2006).

Horrell, David G., Hunt, Cherryl and Southgate, Christopher, *The Green Paul: Rereading the Apostle in an Age of Ecological Crisis* (Waco, TX: Baylor University Press, forthcoming).

Byrne, Brendan (2000), "Creation Groaning: An Earth Bible Reading of Romans 8.18–22", in Norman C. Habel (ed.), *Readings from the Perspective of Earth* (EB 1; Sheffield: Sheffield Academic Press), 193–203.

—— (forthcoming), "An Ecological Reading of Rom 8:19–22: Possibilities and Hesitations", in David G. Horrell, Cherryl Hunt, Christopher Southgate and Francesca Stavrakopoulou (eds), *Ecological Hermeneutics: Biblical, Historical, and Theological Perspectives* (London and New York: T. & T. Clark).

Hunt, Cherryl, Horrell, David G. and Southgate, Christopher, "An Environmental Mantra? Ecological Interest in Romans 8:19–23 and a Modest Proposal for its Narrative Interpretation", *Journal of Theological Studies* 59 (2008) 546–79.

Tonstad, Sigve, "Creation Groaning in Labor Pains", in Norman C. Habel and Peter Trudinger (eds), *Exploring Ecological Hermeneutics* (SBL Symposium Series; Atlanta: Society of Biblical Literature, 2008), 141–49.

Hunt, Cherryl, "Beyond Anthropocentrism: Towards a Re-reading of Pauline Ethics", *Theology* 112 (2009) 190–98.

Balabanski, Vicky, "Critiquing Anthropocentric Cosmology: Retrieving a Stoic 'Permeation Cosmology' in Colossians 1:15–20", in Norman C. Habel and Peter Trudinger (eds), *Exploring Ecological Hermeneutics* (SBL Symposium Series 46; Atlanta, GA: Society of Biblical Literature, 2008), 151–59.

—— "Hellenistic Cosmology and the Letter to the Colossians: Towards an Ecological Hermeneutic", in David G. Horrell, Cherryl Hunt, Christopher Southgate and Francesca Stavrakopoulou (eds), *Ecological Hermeneutics: Biblical, Historical, and Theological Perspectives* (London and New York: T. & T. Clark, forthcoming).

Chapter 8

FUTURE VISIONS OF CREATION AT PEACE

In the previous two chapters we have begun, unavoidably, to focus on texts and traditions that are essentially future-orientated, or *eschatological*; that is to say, that they are concerned with God's future transformation of the world. A central early Christian conviction was that this promised future transformation had already begun; the final act in the drama had commenced, announced and inaugurated by the ministry and especially the resurrection of Jesus. Of course, it is not only in the New Testament that we find future visions of the transformation God will bring about. On the contrary, the Hebrew Bible, the Christian Old Testament, contains a range of prophetic visions of the imminent or distant future, visions which influence and inform the New Testament depictions, as we have already seen in the discussions of Jesus and Paul above.

These future visions have an obvious relevance to discussions of ecology and the environment, for at least two main reasons. First, because discussions of environmental pressures and ethical dilemmas often have a clear future orientation too. Of course, they have a present (and past) dimension as well – in the impact on ecosystems and human welfare that is already evident and measurable, and in the awareness of species already lost forever – but they are often concerned with how to avoid possible future scenarios: how to avoid the most catastrophic effects of global warming, how to preserve endangered species and habitats, and so on. Second, because biblical eschatology, especially as interpreted in some Christian traditions and denominations, seems to raise certain questions about the whole basis for any need to preserve and care for the earth, or to consider the welfare of future generations (see chs 1–2 above). If Jesus might imminently return, and rescue (only) the elect, and if the earth is to be replaced by a new earth (along with a new heaven, as is implied in some of the texts we shall examine), then why bother to protect the environment or conserve future resources? Thinking about what kinds of future visions the Bible offers, and about their possible ecological implications, is, then, a crucial task.

There is another reason why eschatological material needs to be given full and careful consideration, at least in the context of a discussion of the implications of such material for Christian interpreters. Just as eschatological convictions were central to early Christian faith, so they remain fundamental to Christian theology and ethics. While some of the Bible's ethical material has no necessary eschatological frame – such as the command to love of neighbour or other aspects of the Jewish Law – the conviction that God's action in Christ constitutes the decisive event in a plan of salvation is so central to the Christian story that it fundamentally shapes the understanding of what Christian ethics is about. As Helmut Thielicke writes: "Theological ethics is eschatological or it is nothing" (Thielicke 1966: 47). Or, as Victor Paul Furnish writes with regard to Paul, "eschatology is not just one motif among numerous others, but helps to provide the fundamental perspective within which everything else is viewed" (Furnish 1968: 214).

In this chapter and the following one, we shall consider a few examples of these visions, taken from both the Old and New Testaments. I have divided the texts into two types, one to be considered in each chapter. The first type concerns visions of a renewed creation at peace, visions which might, at least in certain respects, seem to offer a rather positive ecological vision of the future. The second type concerns texts which present images of cosmic destruction and therefore immediately raise rather difficult questions for any attempt to derive a positive ecological vision from the Bible. It is important to stress not only that this is, unavoidably, only a restricted treatment of selected texts, but also that the division of the texts into these two types is a somewhat arbitrary decision, not least since the categories and images are blurred and overlapping. In other words, the division into two types, treated separately in these two chapters, does not reflect a division between two recognized types of biblical material, but only a division which is useful in terms of separating two different kinds of ecologically relevant issues that arise.

There is, however, a distinction made by biblical scholars which we should note here concerning types of literary material: the distinction between prophecy and apocalyptic. Broadly speaking, prophecy was a form in which both official figures (e.g. royal court or cult prophets) and unofficial critics voiced oracles or words from God/the gods, in ancient Israel and other contemporary cultures and civilizations. These prophetic declarations were often related to their immediate circumstances and historical context, although sometimes seem to relate to a more remote and distant future (or were certainly later interpreted in this way). Apocalyptic – derived from the Greek word *apokaluptō*, meaning to reveal or uncover – was "the form which prophecy took during the Graeco-Roman period" (Rowland 1990: 34). Apocalyptic literature is characterized by imminent expectation, a strong dualism of good and evil embodied in the contrast between the old age, soon to pass away, and the new eternal age to come, which will be brought in by decisive divine intervention. Apocalyptic "sets out to reveal things as they really are in the world at large" (Rowland 1990: 35); that is, by depicting – often through visionary experiences – what a heavenly perspective shows about the way the world is and about the things that will soon come to pass. Since most scholars would see apocalyptic as a development of the prophetic tradition, it is unsurprising that there is no hard and fast distinction between the two types. And apocalyptic imagery can be used in texts which are not, in terms of their overall type, usually classified as apocalyptic (e.g., Mark 13, discussed in the following chapter). Indeed, one of the prophetic books we shall discuss briefly in both this chapter and the next, Joel, is often seen as standing at the transition between prophecy and apocalyptic. At the very least, Joel seems to represent a collection of prophetic material in which apocalyptic imagery is quite prominent. We turn first, though, to the book of Isaiah.

The renewal of creation in the book of Isaiah

The book of Isaiah has been enormously influential upon Christian theology, from the earliest days. Prophecies concerning a woman bearing a child called Immanuel (Isa. 7:14) and a future ruler, the prince of peace (Isa. 9:6), were quickly interpreted in a messianic way (cf. Matt. 1:23); these texts are well known to Christians as a part of the series of Christmas readings, taken to announce the coming of Christ. And Isaiah's depiction of a suffering servant (Isa. 52:13–53:12) was soon read as a description of the sufferings of Christ (Acts 8:30–35; 1 Pet. 2:21–25). It is likely, however, that these prophecies originally related to the more immediate circumstances of the time. Moreover, scholars have long recognized that the book of Isaiah contains material from a range of historical periods. Consequently, the book has been divided into three main sections: chapters 1–39, stemming, at least in part, from the eighth century BCE, 40–55 and 56–66 reflecting the later context of the return from Exile (sixth century BCE and later). Hence, many scholars refer to Isaiah, Deutero-Isaiah and trito-Isaiah, or use other equivalent terms. Even within each section of the book there is debate about how much of the material might derive from the original historical context of one prophetic figure. While the book can be read as a canonical whole (e.g., Childs 2001), it contains a compilation of materials from a wide variety of contexts and originators.

Among a number of visions of a future peace (under an ideal future ruler) from the first section of the book, Isa. 11:1–9 calls for our attention, due to its inclusion of non-human animals within the scope of this peaceable vision. After a section predicting the rise of a future Davidic ruler, "from the stump of Jesse" (v. 1), who will rule with righteousness and justice (vv. 3–5), the vision continues:

> The wolf shall dwell with the lamb, and the leopard shall lie down with the young goat, and the calf and the lion and the fattened calf together; and a little child shall lead them. The cow and the bear shall graze; their young shall lie down together; and the lion shall eat straw like the ox. The nursing child shall play over the hole of the cobra, and the weaned child shall put his hand on the adder's den. They shall not hurt or destroy in all my holy mountain; for the earth shall be full of the knowledge of the LORD as the waters cover the sea. (Isa. 11:6–9, ESV)

It is uncertain whether these two sections of the vision (vv. 1–5, vv. 6–9) were originally related, but they are clearly brought into close relationship by their juxtaposition in the text: the reign of the anticipated righteous ruler will bring not only social justice (v. 4) but also an end to enmity and violence among animals, and between humans and animals. "The effect of the righteous rule of the Messiah is depicted in terms of an age of universal peace that embraces both the human and animal world" (Childs 2001: 103). Various aspects of the text invite a comparison with the stories in Genesis we have already examined (see chs 3–4). The first creation account in Genesis 1 depicted both animals and humans as originally functioning on a vegetarian/herbivorous diet, a (mythical) vision of pre-history which is here depicted as a future ideal state. And, as Otto Kaiser notes, "if suckling and little child play with the most poisonous snakes, without their mother finding them dead, the old enmity between the seed of the woman and the seed of the snake has been removed (Gen. 3:15)" (Kaiser 1983: 260). So this future peace is, in some ways, depicted as a return to the Edenic paradise.

This vision of peace among the animals is echoed again in Isa. 65:25, using very similar language, and perhaps appears also in Hos. 2:18, but, according to Kaiser, nowhere else in the Old Testament. The description of the good fortunes of the person whom God reproves in the book of Job also includes the theme of peace between humans and animals, with the promise that such a person will "not fear the beasts of the earth. For you shall be in league with the stones of the field, and the beasts of the field shall be at peace with you. You shall know that your tent is at peace, and you shall inspect your fold and miss nothing" (Job 5:22–24, ESV). Kaiser also notes a different tradition, which depicts the peaceable future in a land from which wild animals have been driven away, in order that people may dwell in safety (Ezek. 34:25; Isa. 35:9; Lev. 26:6; cf. Kaiser 1983: 259).

Later Jewish and Jewish-Christian literature also picks up this theme. Philo, the first-century CE Jewish philosopher (*c.* 20 BCE–50 CE), speaking of the need for real obedience to the commands of God and of the enmity between humanity and animals, says that no one can end this enmity, except God, through his election of certain persons as saviours of their race. Philo is here presenting this vision in terms of a philosophically-shaped discussion, focusing on the need for virtuous living. If such good entered the world, he suggests, the wild passions in the human soul would be tamed, and so also would the wild animals:

> Therefore we need not give up hope that when the wild beasts within us are fully tamed the animals too will become tame and gentle. When that time comes I believe that bears and lions and panthers and the Indian animals, elephants and tigers, and all others whose vigour and power are invincible, will change their life of solitariness and isolation for one of companionship, and gradually in imitation of the gregarious creatures show themselves tame when brought face to face with mankind. They will no longer as heretofore be roused to ferocity by the sight, but will be awe-struck into respectful fear of him as their natural lord and master. (Philo, *On Rewards and Punishments* 88–89, trans F. H. Colson)

Philo goes on to describe how venemous creatures will keep their poison inoperative, the river animals that attack people will become tame and gentle, and among the sea creatures "the virtuous man will be sacred and unhurt, since God honours virtue and has given it immunity from all designs against it as a proper reward" (§90, trans C. D. Yonge).

A more direct appropriation of the Isaianic imagery is found in the Sibylline Oracles, a composite Jewish-Christian collection which contains material from a wide range of dates. The third oracle, however, is largely a Jewish composition dating from the second-century and probably originating in Egypt (Collins 1983: 354–55). Speaking of the eschatological kingdom which the great and living God will raise up, the oracle says:

> Wolves and lambs will eat grass together in the mountains. Leopards will feed together with kids. Roving bears will spend the night with calves. The flesh-eating lion will eat husks at the manger like an ox, and mere infant children will lead them with ropes. For he will make the beasts on earth harmless. Serpents and asps will sleep with babies and will not harm them, for the hand of God will be upon them. (*Sib. Or.* 3:788–795, trans J. J. Collins)

As we have already noted (pp. 69–70), Richard Bauckham draws attention to this theme of messianic peace with the animals, suggesting that this tradition underpins and informs the brief reference in Mark 1:13: "he [Jesus] was with the wild animals". Jesus, Bauckham argues, establishes his messianic peace in the wilderness.

It is clear enough (especially in Job 5:24, quoted above), and hardly surprising, in a pre-industrial agricultural economy, that the desire underlying such visions is "the longing for a life with no danger. The fact that the beasts of prey feed with domestic animals means that the farmer will no longer have losses among his herds. If a young child can look after the flocks, being a shepherd has become a peaceful idyll" (Kaiser 1983: 260). In the sixteenth century, Calvin could still depict wild animals as a serious threat to human welfare (see above, p. 46). Yet in a modern Western context, this motif has inspired a different kind of ethical and ecological reflection.

For obvious reasons, Isa. 11:6–9 (and the other related texts), along with Gen. 1:29–30, are particularly significant texts for Christian vegetarians (cf. Webb 2001: 59–81; Linzey 1994: 125–37). The vision of a future (non-predatory) peace is seen as a return to the Creator's original intention; and a commitment to vegetarianism is seen as a way of living eschatologically, in step with, and anticipation of, the realization of God's peaceable kingdom (see Horrell 2008).

From a somewhat different perspective, John Olley finds many of the Earth Bible Project's ecojustice principles (see pp. 13–14) exemplified in the Isaianic material. The many references to animals in the book of Isaiah imply, according to Olley, "the principle of intrinsic worth" (Olley 2001: 221), and the inclusion of animals among those who praise God suggests the principle of voice (p. 222). Furthermore:

> Throughout the book of Isaiah animals are more than recognized as part of the Earth community. Whether wild or domestic, their integrity and diversity is affirmed. The vision of the future worshipping life on the holy mountain includes animals. For Isaiah the distinctive core of the future is not temple worship but an Earth community where all live in mutuality, where all is right and there is no harming or destroying. "Harmful" animals are not banished, rather they share in the transformation with humans (principles of interconnectedness and purpose). All participate in the "knowledge of YHWH" on the "holy mountain". (Olley 2001: 227)

When it comes to the possible present relevance of such visions of the future Olley notes that "prophetic portrayals of the future are not designed merely as predictions or to satisfy curiosity, but rather are means of encouraging appropriate behavioural responses in the present" (p. 228). The force of the Isaianic visions is that "one must respond to a moral claim to do what is possible to minimize violence and enhance harmony now" (p. 229).

An earlier article by Sibley Towner, from which Olley quotes, also sees this prophetic material as a vision of "the transformed ecosystem of the new age": this renewed world is characterized by abundance, peace, long and vigorous life, and an end to death (Towner 1996: 29–30). Because such visions cannot be seen as scientific or historical as such, Towner sees their relevance fundamentally as "moral imperative":

> If peace is the hallmark of the new age (Isa. 11:1–9), then our work in this time of tribulation is to abolish war and to effect reconciliation between people, as well as between people, wolves, and snakes ... The biblical pictures of nature in the future function as incitements toward a style of ethical living in the present that is holistic, interdependent, non-hierarchical, and one that does not reject flesh and matter as corrupt because God does not reject them. (Towner 1996: 33; see also Olley 2001: 229)

Just as Isaiah's vision of a future in which people "beat their swords into ploughshares" (Isa. 2:4) has been a rallying-call for non-violence and pacifism, so one can see how the vision of peace throughout the animal kingdom is an inspiring ecological and ethical vision. Yet, inspiring though this vision might be, there are also difficulties in discerning what its ethical implications ought to be. How is any kind of "reconciliation" between wolves and snakes to be brought about? And how desirable would it be anyway? Does it imply that humans should organize nature into sanitized zoos, where the violence and bloodshed of predation is absent (or at least hidden from view)? As Olley and Towner acknowledge, our scientific understanding of the ways animals function shows us that carnivores simply cannot subsist by eating grass. The insights science has given us into evolution also make it impossible to conceive of an historical time when animals (let alone humans) existed in a pre-predatory herbivorous paradise. The very shape and form of the animals we know – both hunter and hunted – reflect their activity in the chains of predation. Lions would not be lions – have lion-like jaws and lion-like limbs – if they did not hunt prey and tear it apart. Gazelles would not be sleek and swift if they did not have to run from predatory lions.

So this vision of eschatological transformation cannot be achieved, nor is it even desirable to achieve, in the world as we know it. It makes no ecological or ethical sense to envisage a moral imperative to bring predation to an end. It is of course possible for human beings – at least, those with adequate resources and opportunities – to nourish themselves on a vegetarian diet, but there are at least questions to discuss about whether this is the most appropriate ethical response to the call towards peace and reconciliation (cf. Southgate 2008a; Horrell 2008; Pollan 2006: 304–33). Once again we find that material with some apparently positive contribution to make to an ecological theology and ethics does not easily translate into clear instruction or responsibilities. This future vision may indeed inform and inspire an ecological worldview, but will require some careful (and scientifically informed) reflection to do so.

Another important and influential aspect of the future visions of the book of Isaiah is the motif of the new heavens and the new earth. Much material in Deutero-Isaiah (chs 40–55) offers a rich and varied portrait of the renewal and restoration into which God is leading the people, a redemption generally associated with the return from exile facilitated by the Persian ruler Cyrus in the sixth-century BCE (see Isa. 45:1). Along with an insistence on Yhwh as the incomparably great creator (e.g., 42:5–8; 43:10–21) and a polemic against the "idols" which other peoples worship (e.g., 44:9–18), we find reference to the "new thing" God is doing (Isa. 43:18–19). This idea is often seen as an influence on the more specific motif of the "new heavens and new earth", found explicitly in Isa. 65:17: "For behold, I create new heavens and a new earth, and the former things shall not be remembered or come into mind" (ESV; cf. also Isa. 66:22). Similar phrases occur in later Jewish and early Christian literature, such as "new creation", found in *Jubilees* 4:26, *1 Enoch* 72:1, and in 2 Cor. 5:17 and Gal. 6:15 (these latter two being the only occurrences of "new creation" as a phrase in the entire Bible). These phrases evidently refer to some kind of eschatological transformation. Scholars disagree about whether the references in Paul, for example, refer primarily to the transformation (through conversion) of the individual believer (so Hubbard 2002) or to the cosmic new age inaugurated by the death and resurrection of Christ (so Mell 1989). What is also of particular relevance for ecological interpretation is to consider whether this image of eschatological transformation implies the end of the current earth or rather its renewal. We shall consider this question, among others, when we turn shortly to the book of Revelation, where the Isaianic phrase "new heaven and new earth" is used to describe the culmination of the seer's vision. However, first we turn briefly to the book of Joel.

Restoration of the land in the book of Joel

The book of the prophet Joel, part of the "book of the twelve" in the Hebrew Bible, sometimes called "the minor prophets", is a rather enigmatic and difficult book. Scholars disagree over whether it should be seen as a unity or as a collection of diverse material, perhaps from various periods. The date and context are also uncertain, though most scholars favour a date in the post-exilic (Persian) period (see Barton 2001: 4–18). Whatever one's conclusions about unity and date, it is widely agreed that there is a basic division between 1:1–2.27 and 2:28–3:21 (Barton 2001: 5–14). The latter section, with its distinctive eschatological imagery, will be considered in the following chapter. We are concerned here with the opening sections of the book, and with 2:18–27 in particular.

The opening sections of Joel present a repeated pattern in which some situation of disaster is presented, followed by a call to rituals of lament and an expression of lament. John Barton sees the structure of this repeated cycle in 1:2–2:17 as follows (Barton 2001: 14; cf. Mason 1994: 99):

1:2–4	Details of disaster	2:1–11	Details of disaster
1:5–14	Call to lament	2:12–17a	Call to lament
1:15–20	The lament	2:17bc	The lament

The first depiction of disaster is of a plague of locusts, perhaps intended literally, or perhaps intended as an image of an army's invasion (cf. 1:6); the second presents images of fire, horses, chariots, and so on, to depict in apocalyptic terms the invasion of an army, associated with a terrible "day of the Lord". While some have seen these two disasters as different events, Barton argues strongly that the two descriptions relate to the same enemy, the locusts: "What is predicted is a perfectly literal locust invasion, described with magnificent poetic hyperbole" (p. 70).

A striking aspect of these depictions of disaster is the devastation of the land: "The fields are devastated, the ground mourns; for the grain is destroyed, the wine dries up, the oil fails" (1:10, NRSV). This is, of course, entirely understandable as a prominent and, for the people, life-threatening consequence of the locust plague (note the prominent references to agricultural produce in 1:10–12, 16–20). But this motif of the land/earth mourning is encountered in a number of places in the prophetic literature (Isa. 24:1–20; 33:9; Jer. 4:28; 12:4, 11; 23:10; Amos 1:2; Hos. 4:3; see Hayes 2002; Braaten 2008: 68). This reflects a theme we have already noted, namely the extent to which the fortunes of the land are seen as inextricably bound up with the changing state of human fortunes. As Katherine Hayes suggests, "the metaphor of earth mourning can be seen as conveying a theological message about the interrelationship of human beings, God, and the cosmos" (2002: 243). When humans become corrupt or degraded, or turn away from God, animals and the land become degraded and devastated too (cf. Gen. 3–8; ch. 4 above). When humans are restored and righteous, the land flourishes and is fertile (cf. Isa. 11:1–9, discussed above). Here in Joel, the prophet depicts the threat – or the reality – of a time of devastation and famine. For any society, such problems are calamitous, and are understood here as God's doing. Consequently, the prophet calls for rituals of lament (1:13–14; 2:12–13) which may hopefully lead to God's mercy, and consequent restoration (2:14). Interestingly, Joel (unlike some of the other prophets) does not specify any way in which the people have sinned as such, though 2:13 might imply that they need to repent. Perhaps the fact of devastation of the land is, by itself, indication of a situation of desperate need, when the people need to mourn and lament, in the hope of bringing about an act of restoration and mercy on God's part (cf. 2:18).

In an explicitly ecological reading of these chapters, Laurie Braaten takes this argument further. In Joel 1, he suggests,

> Earth and God (through the prophet) clearly mourn the crisis at hand, yet the people have not yet responded … Earth is suffering and mourns. In the process, Earth serves as a model for proper human mourning, and calls for humans to identify with Earth's suffering. Earth also condemns human sin; Earth's suffering stands as a sign to humans that they have not repented of the damage they have done to Earth … Earth has suffered collateral damage in God's judgment against human sin. (Braaten 2008: 68–70; cf. also Braaten 2006)

Certainly one may see in this passage, from a modern ecological perspective, a strong sense of the "interconnectedness" of all the members of the earth community, human and non-human (cf. p. 14 above). This text (and others) powerfully depicts a devastation that affects the whole land and (thus) affects humans too, and also implies that human response, in the form of a turning or appeal to God, may reverse this dreadful fate. But it is perhaps less convincing to see in this text any explicit indication that humans have damaged the earth (the locusts are the prime culprit here), or that their sin – hardly specified or mentioned here, as we have noted – is exposed and condemned. And while the image of earth mourning is indeed a provocative and powerful one, it is perhaps stretching a point to try and see here any indication that this is presented as a "model for proper human mourning", and that earth leads the way where stubborn humans need to go – towards a proper expression of lament and repentance.

These depictions of disaster and lament are followed in 2:18–27 by God's response, in which the people are promised a restoration of their fortunes and a recompense for "the years that the swarming locust has eaten" (2.25). "All the destruction that was foretold in the preceding material now goes into reverse: the pastures grow green again; the fig trees and vines yield fruit; and there is rain once more" (Barton 2001: 89). As Barton notes, the address, "Be not afraid ... be glad", is directed first to the land (2:21), then to the animals (2:22), and then to the people (2:23). In this positive vision of restoration, as in the negative depiction of mourning and lament, the land is a central character, fully active in both mourning and rejoicing. As with the motif of creation's praise, explored in Chapter 5, this is certainly a theme that invites ecological reflection. Not only is there a profound sense of interconnectedness – land, animals and humans bound up in a common and connected fate – but also a sense of earth as a character, addressed, valued, and transformed by God. Far from a vision of salvation for human souls, rescued from a corrupt and expendable material realm, this kind of vision is one of holistic transformation, with the restoration of land and people inextricably part of what future hope entails.

Yet at the same time as these are thought-provoking and ecologically relevant images, it should equally be clear how far they reflect the context and concerns of an agriculturally-focused ancient society where the struggle for subsistence was an everyday issue for the vast majority. After all, just as the depiction of the land's destitution focuses on its lack of produce (1:5–20), so too the picture of its flourishing is clearly anthropocentric, stressing the fertility and bounty which will result in the people having plenty to eat (2:26). The emphasis falls firmly on the land's productivity and plentiful yields, so it is hard to say that the ecojustice value of the "intrinsic worth" of all things is evident here; it is the value of the land for humans that is most strongly apparent.

New heaven and new earth in the book of Revelation

The Christian Bible opens with the creation accounts of the book of Genesis (see ch. 3 above) and closes with the book of Revelation and its vision of the new Jerusalem descending from heaven to earth (Rev. 21:1–22:5). Once again there are motifs that tie these depictions together: the tree of life and the river (22:1–2, cf. Gen. 2:10), the promise of an end to pain and death (Rev. 21:4, cf. Gen. 2:17; 3:3, 16–19). The new Jerusalem is, as John Sweet comments, "paradise regained" (Sweet 1979: 308). The book of Revelation as a whole, as its opening phrase implies, is an example of apocalyptic literature: "the revelation (Gk *apokalupsis*) of Jesus Christ", given to John (1:1). Full of enigmatic imagery, it depicts the cosmic conflict between the power of God and the Lamb and the power of the dragon and the beast, showing the things that must unfold as God's final and ultimate victory is brought about. This imagery, mysterious and difficult as it is, has, of course, fostered a huge array of interpretation through the ages (see Kovacs and Rowland 2004). Precisely because it is full of images and coded depictions, the book allows readers to apply its symbolism to whatever threats and oppositions they currently encounter: the Pope, the Communist countries of the (now former) Soviet Union, the new American empire, and so on (see Hays 1997: 170–71).

The final vision, of "a new heaven and a new earth" (21:1), at the centre of which stands the new Jerusalem, is, of course, enormously influential in Christian tradition and hymnody. In this future vision we again find inspiring and hopeful words, depicting a coming existence free from suffering and hardship:

> And I heard a loud voice from the throne saying, "See, the home of God is among mortals. He will dwell with them; they will be his peoples, and God himself will be with them; he will wipe every tear from their eyes. Death will be no more; mourning and crying and pain will be no more, for the first things have passed away." (Rev. 21:3–4, NRSV)

In the context of the present study, focused on the ecological implications of biblical texts, one key question is whether this vision is, or can be interpreted as, a positive ecological vision of the earth's future. Does the description of a "new heaven and a new earth" imply that the old earth is simply destined for destruction, a temporary home from which humanity may hope to be redeemed? And what kind of place is the new Jerusalem intended to be?

In a discussion of these closing chapters of the book of Revelation, under the heading of the question, "What does God's good future look like?", Steven Bouma-Prediger argues that a positive ecological vision does emerge (Bouma-Prediger 2001: 110–16). He makes a number of claims based on this text: "First, God's good future is earthy. It includes a renewed heaven and earth" (p. 114). Indeed, we might add, the vision is not one in which people get taken up into heaven, but one where the city from heaven descends to be on the earth (21:2–3). The "new heaven and new earth" does not, Bouma-Prediger argues, imply the destruction of the old cosmos and the emergence of a new one, but rather "connotes new in quality" (p. 114). Bouma-Prediger quotes from the commentary of Eugene Boring:

> Even though the first earth and the first heaven have passed away, the scene
> continues very much as a this-worldly scene … The advent of the heavenly
> city does not abolish all human efforts to build a decent earthly civilisation
> but fulfills them. God does not make "all new things," but "all things new"
> (21:5). (Bouma-Prediger 2001: 114, quoting Boring 1989: 220)

Second, "in God's good future God himself will dwell with us and all our
creaturely kin" (p. 114; cf. Rev. 21:3). Furthermore, the separation between
heaven and earth is overcome, and evil and its consequences are no more
(pp. 114–15). And the new, holy city is "a most unusual city":

> The holy city is precisely that – holy – for God is everywhere … nothing in
> this city is profane; nothing is not sacred. All is for the service of God. And
> this city is a gardened city. In this city flows the crystalline river of life,
> watering (among other things) trees that line its banks … People of all kinds
> stream into this city, whose gates never close and whose light never ceases.
> (p. 115)

Thus, in the words of George Caird, it is the most eloquent statement in
the New Testament of "the all-embracing scope of God's redemptive work"
(p. 115, quoting Caird 1966: 280). So, Bouma-Prediger proposes, this is "an
earthly vision of life made good and whole and right, because of God's
grace. Heaven and earth are renewed and are one. God dwells with us, at
home in creation … In short, a world of shalom" (pp. 115–16). Finally, he
quotes George Caird's comment on the phrase "making all things new"
(Rev. 21:5):

> This is not an activity of God within the new creation, after the old has been
> cast as rubbish to the void; it is the process of re-creation by which the old is
> transformed into the new. In Smyrna and Thyatira, in Sardis and Laodicea, in
> all places of his dominion, God is forever making all things new, and on this
> depends the hope of the world. (p. 116, quoting Caird 1966: 265–66)

However, in this positive ecological reconstruction, certain aspects of the
vision have been somewhat overlooked. Stressing the continuity rather
than discontinuity – renewal not replacement – is somewhat difficult given
the statement that "the first heaven and the first earth had passed away",
and that the new creation no longer has any sea (21:1) nor any night (21:25).
This new creation, then, has to be radically different from the functioning
earth-systems as we know them. Moreover, the focus of the new heaven
and earth is overwhelmingly urban, with the detailing of impressive
measurements showing how vast is the city's size and scale (21:16–21). It is
cubic in shape, extending for around 1,500 miles in each direction – truly

a megalopolis if ever there were one! What is more, immoral people (and dogs!) are firmly excluded from the city (21:8, 27; 22:15).

Duncan Reid is somewhat more candid about the ambivalent ecological legacy of this text, but also argues that renewal rather than replacement is its theme: "This world is not 'raw material' to be annihilated in the process, but is honoured in the new creation that descends from 'heaven' to transform and renew the earth" (Reid 2000: 242). Reid acknowledges that the vision is "anthropocentric" and that "[t]he new Jerusalem is not an ecological city" (p. 243). However, he suggests that "we need not read this simply as a neglect of 'nature' for two reasons":

> First, cities are never without non-human plant and animal life, both domestic and wild. It is quite probable that this non-human presence is simply assumed in the description of the new Jerusalem ... Secondly ... the notion of an "eco-city" tends to colonize "nature" by rendering it safe and tame... Revelation 21–22 refuses just this temptation. For all its vast size, the new Jerusalem does have its limits, its city walls ... And though wild non-human creatures may well be found within the walls – as they are in any ancient or modern city – there is a preserve for non-human creation beyond the walls. No city exists without its hinterland, and the non-human creation is surely there, enjoying its own domain. It is afforded a respectful textual silence in Revelation; the silence underlines that non-human nature is free – it has not been assimilated into the urban, human habitat. (Reid 2000: 243–44)

There are no particular reasons, however, for reading the author's silence as "respectful"; it is simply silence. John has no interest in the animals and plants, the "non-human creation" that might – or might not – be "enjoying its own domain" outside the city. The vision, as with the others we have considered, is shaped by its context. In the context of an agricultural or pastoral community, Isaiah and Joel presented visions that related to the most obvious desires and needs of the people: for an end to the threat to livestock and people from marauding predators and poisonous snakes, for fertile ground and bountiful production. John, writing to the urban churches in the province of Asia (near the Western coast of present-day Turkey), envisioned a city of God that would far exceed the riches and glory of Rome's most extravagant constructions. John's vision might be of some relevance to questions of urban planning – though his philosophy would seem to be that "big is beautiful" – but does not directly convey any ecological vision for the whole earth.

Conclusion

Many interpreters, keen to avoid the implication that John's vision might support an anti-ecological view of earth as a temporary domain to be cast away and replaced, have, as we have seen in the examples above, stressed that the vision is one of transformation, not replacement. This is seen as a crucial point to stress in recovering a positive ecological theology and ethics from the Bible (cf. also ch. 9 below). In a broader study of the motif of the "new heavens and new earth", for example, David Russell states that:

> The apocalyptists and biblical writers anticipated the renewal of creation. However, this hope did not reflect negatively upon the *present* natural order. Indeed, it actually affirmed its significance as a part of God's redemptive plan ... God is both creator *and* redeemer who has not abandoned his creation but fully intends to bring it to fulfillment ... Christians who take seriously their participation in God's *cosmic* work of salvation must so order their lives in accordance with this universal scope of redemption ... God's creation is worth preserving, and whatever the transformation of the new heavens and the new earth may involve, it includes primarily a cleansing of all that opposes God and perverts creation's purpose. (Russell 1996: 210, 212–13)

Likewise, in a study of evangelical eschatologies and the environment, Thomas Finger puts considerable effort into showing that the biblical texts imply significant continuity between old and new creation, on the assumption that "[i]f the present creation will not be destroyed but renewed, it would seem important to care for it today" (Finger 1998: 1; cf. also Lucas 1999; Moo 2006). However, it is not so clear that a vision of transformation is necessarily more ecologically positive and relevant. We have already briefly touched on this issue in relation to Rom. 8:19–23 (see ch. 7). Even if we accept that the "new heaven and new earth" stand in some continuity with the existing (heaven and) earth, and that the old will not simply be cast away, the transformation in view is so radical that it changes the world into something utterly removed from the world of our experience. Lions will eat straw; no-one will die. And this transformation is something that God – and only God – can and will bring about. Not only does this imply that God can and will bring about this (re)new(ed) creation whatever mess humans have made of the old one, but also that such a radically different creation cannot be achieved by any amount of eco-friendly action on the part of humans. Does this then imply that the visions of future peace and fertility, of a bountiful earth and renewed creation, cannot shape an ecological theology and inform an ecological ethics? Once again, I do not intend to imply that this is the case. But the difficulties and questions should at least alert us to the fact that such a theology and ethics are not simply to be found within the pages of the Bible. Indeed, when we turn in the next chapter to a rather different set of future visions, the difficulties become all the more apparent.

Further reading

Mason, Rex, *Zephaniah, Habakkuk, Joel* (OTG; Sheffield: Sheffield Academic Press, 1994).

Barton, John, *Isaiah 1–39* (OTG; Sheffield: Sheffield Academic Press, 1995).

Bauckham, Richard J., *The Theology of the Book of Revelation* (New Testament Theology; Cambridge: CUP, 1993).

Olley, John W., "'The Wolf, the Lamb, and a Little Child': Transforming the Diverse Earth Community in Isaiah", in Norman C. Habel (ed.), *The Earth Story in the Psalms and the Prophets* (EB 4; Sheffield: Sheffield Academic Press, 2001), 219–29.

Towner, W. Sibley, "The Future of Nature", *Interpretation* 50 (1996) 27–35.

Bouma-Prediger, Steven, *For the Beauty of the Earth: A Christian Vision for Creation Care* (Grand Rapids, MI: Baker Academic, 2001), 110–16.

Reid, Duncan (2000), "Setting Aside the Ladder to Heaven: Revelation 21:1–22:5 from the Perspective of the Earth", in Norman C. Habel (ed.), *Readings from the Perspective of Earth* (EB 1; Sheffield: Sheffield Academic Press), 232–45.

Chapter 9

APOCALYPTIC VISIONS OF COSMIC CATASTROPHE

In the previous chapter we considered some examples of texts which depict creation in the future, renewed and at peace. Although these texts offer visions of the future which are in some ways ecologically inspiring and can perhaps function to inform moral goals, they also raise difficult questions about how such depictions can translate into policies and practices relevant and meaningful to the "real" world. The kind of visions we shall examine in this chapter raise even more difficult questions, since they depict catastrophic and cataclysmic events on a cosmic scale as part of the future eschatological scenario, events that will herald the arrival of the new creation or the new heaven and new earth. As we saw in Chapter 2, when surveying the various approaches to interpreting the Bible in relation to ecological issues, these texts may support, or may be used to support, a form of Christian eschatology which stresses the possibility of Jesus' imminent return, a return which will be heralded by signs of cosmic collapse and lead to the salvation of the human elect. If this is the Christian hope, it may be argued, then those who call for environmental care may be working against God's purposes, since they are trying (in vain, of course) to delay the process by which the End will come. So just as the Bible's opening story of creation, with its mandate for human dominion over the earth (see ch. 3), raises difficulties for an ecological theology, so too do the Bible's visions of the future, especially those which envision some form of cosmic catastrophe as the necessary prelude to the arrival of the new creation.

In this chapter I shall first present a brief survey of three examples of such texts of cosmic catastrophe; this will help to indicate what the key issues and difficulties are, and the extent to which the texts do or do not support the kind of fundamentalist reading mentioned briefly above (and in ch. 2). I shall then illustrate the different approaches to interpreting such material among biblical scholars and ecological writers. Finally, I shall consider some of the possible ways of handling this material, in the context of our attempt to assess the Bible's contribution to our thinking about issues of ecology and the environment.

"Portents in the heavens and on the earth": Joel 2:28–3:21

In the previous chapter we have already considered some aspects of the visions of the renewal of the land in the book of Joel (esp. 2:18–27). The future visions of the book continue again from 2:28 onwards, and whether commentators read this as part of a unified continuation of the same prophetic work (e.g., Coggins 2000: 17–19) or as a later collection of oracles (Barton 2001: 5–14, 92–93), most agree that a distinct section, with new imagery, begins here. The sayings collected in this final section of the book do not appear to have a clear or coherent thread (cf., e.g., 2:28–29 and 2:30–31), and some bear a close relationship to what are probably earlier oracles in other prophetic books (cf., e.g., 3:10 with Isa. 2:4; Mic. 4:3), but, at least in parts, the eschatological imagery here becomes more apocalyptic in character.

As with the earlier sections of the book, the focus is on the people of Israel (3:2, 16), centred on Jerusalem (2:32; 3:1, 6, 16, 20), and the future restoration of their fortunes. The images of cosmic catastrophe depict what will accompany "the great and terrible day of the Lord" (2:31), a day of judgement and reckoning (3:1–15), which will lead to a time of salvation, peace and fertility in the land (3:18–20). It is clear that these images of fertility and plenty are tied to a vision of Israel's vindication and restoration: Judah's "mountains shall drip with sweet wine and the hills shall flow with milk", while "Egypt shall become a desolation and Edom a desolate wilderness" (3:18–19, NRSV).

The images that particularly call for our attention in this chapter are found in 2:30–31 and 3:15–16:

> I will show portents in the heavens and on the earth, blood and fire and columns of smoke. The sun shall be turned to darkness, and the moon to blood, before the great and terrible day of the LORD comes. (2:30–31)

> The sun and the moon are darkened, and the stars withdraw their shining. The LORD roars from Zion, and utters his voice from Jerusalem, and the heavens and the earth shake. (3:15–16, NRSV)

As John Barton notes, "[t]here is a long prophetic tradition identifying the darkening of the sky as a portent of disaster in the human world" (Barton 2001: 98, citing Isa. 13:10; 34:4; Jer. 4:23; Ezek. 32:7–8; Amos 8:9). The images of blood, fire and smoke, Barton suggests, might imply either "natural disaster (perhaps earthquake or volcanic eruption) or invasion and war" (p. 98). More than this, the signs of cosmic collapse – the darkening of the sun, and so on – together with the shaking of the heavens and the earth, imply "that the stability of the whole established world is under threat" (Adams 2007: 47). Yet through and beyond this time of upheaval and judgement, God's people are assured of protection and salvation (3:16–21).

"Heaven and earth will pass away": Mark 13

Imagery from Joel, and from other Jewish texts (such as the book of Daniel) is taken up in Mark 13 (paralleled in Matt. 24:1–44 and Luke 21:5–36). In this section of Mark, sometimes known as the Markan apocalypse, Jesus utters his longest section of teaching in the Gospel, in response to his disciples' observation about the temple. There are many complex questions about the sources, historicity and meaning of this discourse (see Adams 2007: 133–66; Yarbro Collins 2007: 591–619). Most scholars, though not all, take it to refer both to the destruction of the temple in 70 CE – an event thought to be either already complete or at least inevitable when Mark wrote – and to the future coming (Gk *parousia*) of the Son of Man, identified with Jesus the Messiah. As Morna Hooker puts it:

> The fact that Mark puts two questions into the mouths of the disciples in v. 4 and separates the events in Judaea from the cosmic events in vv. 24–7, suggests that he regards the two as linked together, yet not identical ... Mark seems to regard it [the destruction of Jerusalem in 70 CE] as the beginning of the tribulation which will continue till the End arrives ... The temple's desolation was the sign of disaster and destruction for Israel, but it was not the End of all things. Of that End there will be no more signs until the heavens themselves presage the arrival of the Son of man. (Hooker 1991: 302–03)

Again, natural and human disasters are seen as a necessary part of the sequence of events that will herald the dawning of these eschatological times: earthquakes, wars and famines (Mk 13:7–8). Most relevant for our concerns is a section in which the imagery of cosmic catastrophe, reminiscent of Joel and other earlier texts, appears once more:

> But in those days, after that suffering, the sun will be darkened, and the moon will not give its light, and the stars will be falling from heaven, and the powers in the heavens will be shaken. (Mk 13:24–25, NRSV)

At this time of crisis, the Son of Man will come, and send his angels to "gather his elect from the four winds, from the ends of the earth to the ends of heaven" (13:27). And when Jesus assures his listeners that "this generation will not pass away until all these things have taken place", he insists that "heaven and earth will pass away, but my words will not pass away" (13:30–31).

"The heavens will pass away": 2 Peter 3:10–13

In the second letter of Peter, widely seen as one of the later letters of the New Testament, probably not written by Peter himself but at some point after his death, the author responds to "scoffers" who doubt that the promised coming of the Lord will ever materialize (2 Pet. 3:3). The key arguments of these so-called scoffers would seem to be that the time when the promise should have been fulfilled is now past and that the world continues as it always has done, with no sign or likelihood of dramatic divine intervention (3:4). The author responds to these arguments with counterarguments of his own. He insists that God's timescale is not the same as that of humans (3:8–9, drawing on Ps. 90:4). More significantly, he counters the notion that the world is destined to continue as a stable system by appealing first to God's creation of the world "out of water and by means of water" (3:5) and second to God's subsequent destruction of that world with water (3:6), alluding, of course, to the flood story of Genesis 6–8. This previous cycle of events serves, in the author's view, to establish a pattern that will be repeated, this time through a destruction by fire. In each case the action is done "by the word of God".

> But by the same word the present heavens and earth have been reserved for fire, being kept until the day of judgment and destruction of the godless. (3:7, NRSV).

This time of fiery destruction is associated with the day of judgement and the day of the Lord, as is the imagery of destruction in Joel and other prophetic texts.

> But the day of the Lord will come like a thief, and then the heavens will pass away with a loud noise, and the elements will be dissolved with fire, and the earth and everything that is done on it will be disclosed. (3:10, NRSV)

Finally, the author appeals to this pattern of future events as a reason for his readers to live holy and godly lives,

waiting for and hastening the coming of the day of God, because of which the
heavens will be set ablaze and dissolved, and the elements will melt with fire
... But, in accordance with his promise, we wait for new heavens and a new
earth, where righteousness is at home. (3:12–13, NRSV)

There are many difficult exegetical questions concerning these verses (see
Adams 2007: 200–35; Bauckham 1983: 303–26, for full discussions). But
two aspects of the text are particularly noteworthy and relevant here. One
is the depiction of a coming destruction of the cosmos by fire. Drawing on
both biblical traditions and on Stoic cosmology – which envisaged periodic
destruction and reconstitution of the cosmos by water and by fire – the
author emphasizes that a future destruction of the world is coming, a
destruction analogous in some ways to the destruction wrought by the
Noachic flood. The second is the appeal to readers to "hasten the day",
through their holy and godly living. God is delaying the day of reckoning
out of patience for the ungodly, but believers should live in a way that will
hasten its arrival, since after the fiery destruction comes a "new heavens
and a new earth, where righteousness is at home" (3:13).

Interpreting texts of cosmic catastrophe

It is clear, then, at least on an initial reading, that some biblical texts, like
the examples we have briefly surveyed above, present a vision of cosmic
catastrophe and cataclysm as part of the final day of judgement and prelude
to the arrival of the new age of righteousness and peace. Some, like Mark
13, refer also to the rescue of the elect (cf. also 1 Thess. 4:13–5:11), or in
various ways assure the righteous people of God of their safety and future
blessing through and beyond this time of judgement and transformation
(Joel 3:16–21). One can understand why some Christians take these texts
to inform a set of eschatological hopes which focus on the imminent return
of Jesus (cf. Mk 13:30; 2 Pet. 3:9–10), the rescue of the elect (cf. Mk 13:27),
and the destruction of the old earth, the old heavens, and all the wicked
and ungodly (2 Pet. 3:7, 10, 12). What does this mean for any attempt to
find biblical support for environmental care? What are the alternatives for
interpreting these texts?

One way to make sense of the imagery of cosmic catastrophe is to regard
it as an established set of Jewish metaphors for depicting a time of
momentous socio-political change. N. T. Wright is a prominent
contemporary proponent of this interpretative option (see esp. Wright
1999). For Wright, the apocalyptic language depicting a contrast between
this age and the age to come does not refer to the literal "end" of the space-

time universe. When first-century Jews and early Christians "used what we might call cosmic imagery to describe the coming new age, such language cannot be read in a crassly literalistic way without doing it great violence ... The 'kingdom of god' has nothing to do with the world itself coming to an end" (Wright 1992: 284–85). What is envisaged is "an end to the *present world order*", not the "end of the space-time world" (p. 299); "the eschatological expectation of most Jews of this period was for a renewal, not an abandonment, of the present space-time order as a whole" (pp. 331–32). Discussing Mark 13 in particular, Wright proposes:

> It is crass literalism, in view of the many prophetic passages in which this language denotes socio-political and military catastrophe, to insist that this time the words must refer to the physical collapse of the space-time world. This is simply the way regular Jewish imagery is able to refer to major socio-political events and bring out their full significance ... The reference to heaven and earth passing away must not, of course, be taken as an indication that the discourse has after all been about the end of the space-time universe, but as another typical Jewish metaphor. (Wright 1996: 361, 364; cf. 1999: 9)

What Mark 13 is essentially about, then, is the destruction of Jerusalem and its temple, and the (related) vindication of Jesus and his followers. The language of cosmic catastrophe is used to depict, in vivid and established metaphorical terms, the earth-shattering consequences of such a historical moment.

Similar in some ways to Wright's interpretation, though presenting a very different socio-political reading of Mark, Ched Myers also argues that we should interpret Mark 13 as a depiction of historical transformation, not the end of the world as we know it. Since the age to come overlaps with the present age, this cannot be a matter of chronology, as if a new world were set to replace the present one (cf. Myers 1988: 338). "Mark advocates neither fatalism nor escapism, but a revolutionary commitment to the transformation of history, which always demands political vigilance and discernment ... [he] envisions the renewal of *everything* in the universe" (pp. 341, 344).

For obvious reasons, those seeking to find ecological wisdom in the Bible tend to favour something like this kind of interpretation, stressing that the imagery of cosmic catastrophe and imminent end does not imply the rejection and destruction of the existing earth, but rather its renewal. While Mark 13 raises certain difficulties in this regard, 2 Peter 3 is widely recognized as the most "difficult" example. Nonetheless, arguments are mounted to show that it, too, emphasizes renewal not destruction.

Richard Bauckham, commenting on 2 Pet. 3:13, accepts that "[s]uch passages emphasize the radical discontinuity between the old and the new, but it is nevertheless clear that they intend to describe a renewal, not an abolition, of creation" (Bauckham 1983: 326). In an essay on "New Testament teaching on the environment", Ernest Lucas confronts the apparent difficulties of 2 Peter 3. First, Lucas notes that the most likely reading of 3:10 is not that the earth will be "burned up", as some manuscripts and English translations have it, but that it will be "found", or exposed for judgement (cf. NRSV, ESV; Lucas 1999: 97). Second, he argues that the "elements" (Gk *stoicheia*) in 3:10 refers not to the physical universe, but to spiritual powers or heavenly beings. More generally, he argues that the author is likely using "figurative" language about cosmic events: "Hence we should be wary of reading it as a literal account of the end of the physical cosmos". The primary focus is on God's judgement, for which the metaphor of fire is used in the Old Testament (p. 97). And since the author uses the Greek word *kainos* (new in quality) rather than *neos* (new in the sense of previously non-existent), Lucas argues that "although 2 Peter 3 is speaking of a radical transformation of the heaven and the earth, it is a renewal through transformation, not a total destruction of the old and its replacement by something quite different". Thus, Lucas argues, "[i]t is certainly not a basis for arguing against Christian concern for, and involvement in, ecological issues" (p. 97).

A similar defence of 2 Peter 3 is mounted by Steven Bouma-Prediger (see also Finger 1998: 3–6). Like Lucas, Bouma-Prediger notes that many translations render 2 Pet. 3:10 as a reference to the earth being "burned up". He sees this as "perhaps the most egregious mistranslation in the entire New Testament" (Bouma-Prediger 2001: 77). This hyperbolic comment does not do justice to the fact that it is more a textual than a translational question (cf. Bouma-Prediger 2001: 196 n. 43), since some ancient manuscripts – including those that represent the established Byzantine tradition reflected in the KJV, etc. – do read *katakaēsetai* ("will be burned up"), while others read *heurethēsetai* ("will be found"). It is indeed much more likely that this latter word represents the original text (cf. Bauckham 1983: 303). So, Bouma-Prediger asserts, "the text rightly rendered speaks of a basic continuity rather than discontinuity of this world with the next ... Biblical eschatology affirms the redemption and restoration of creation" (p. 77).

Such attempts at what we have labelled readings of recovery (see ch. 2) are not, however, the only ecologically orientated approach to these texts. In an essay in the Earth Bible series, Keith Dyer presents an attempt "to retrieve some of these 'texts of cosmic terror' from the grip of both fanatical and scholarly apocalypticism, to re-evaluate them in light of Earth Bible principles, and to wrestle with those texts that seem to persist as words against Earth" (Dyer 2002: 44). After outlining a set of "biblicist eschatological principles" (quoted on p. 11 above), Dyer turns to issues in the interpretation of Mark 13. Challenging what he calls the "distorting polarities" of the modern "apocalyptic paradigm" – an approach which stresses dualities between earth and heaven, present and future – he argues that "[t]he cosmic events of Mk 13:24–25 can be understood ... as reflecting the falling leaders and powers immediately preceding Mark's day" (Dyer 2002: 52). "All these things" (Mk 13:30) refers to a series of events "in the recent memory and current experience of the Markan community" (p. 53).

However, despite his belief that some aspects of Mark 13 can be "retrieved", other parts of the text, Dyer proposes, cannot plausibly be read as earth-friendly. Mark 13:31 – "heaven and earth will pass away" – "does affirm the prerogative of the Creator to decreate the cosmos" (p. 54). And even if the language of 2 Peter 3 can be taken to refer to the renewal of earth rather than its annihilation and replacement, it still "presents insurmountable problems for a retrieval of the text from the perspective of Earth ... since [such texts] also exhort the hearer to actively desiring, if not hastening (2 Pet. 3:13), that day. Texts that at the most maintain the prerogative of the Creator to de-/re-create the creation (Mk 13:31; Rev. 21:1) here have become texts that encourage our eager expectation of, and even participation in, that process" (p. 55; cf. also pp. 48–49).

The more negative conclusions to which Dyer comes are broadly reinforced and developed much further in an important and comprehensive study of New Testament texts of cosmic catastrophe by Edward Adams (2007). Setting these texts in the context of Jewish and Greco-Roman literature and thought, Adams argues that texts like Mark 13 and 2 Peter 3 (and others, such as Heb. 12:25–29 and Rev. 6:12–27), do depict the real collapse and disintegration of the present cosmos. Adams stresses that this does not imply the complete annihilation of the earth, since this was not a conceivable option within the categories of first-century cosmology. But it does mean that this is not merely imagery describing momentous socio-political transformation, whatever we might wish. 2 Peter 3, in particular, Adams argues, is influenced by the Stoic doctrine of cosmic conflagration, in which the cosmos is reduced to its basic elements and then reconstituted. In a sense this is indeed a renewal rather than an annihilation, a "recycling" of the elements of the universe, but it is a renewal which involves a destructive end followed by a reconstitution (Adams 2007: 200–35).

Possible strategies for ecological interpretation

What then are the possible ways of interpreting these texts and of dealing with their theological and ethical implications?

One way is to accept, along with Adams, that these texts really do depict a coming cosmic catastrophe, an effective end for the present earth. As we have seen, the texts which add to this an appeal for believers to "hasten" the day only increase the difficulties for any reading orientated to valuing and preserving the earth. But, lest we think 2 Peter's language here injects a particularly pernicious difficulty, it is worth pointing out that *any* eschatological vision of hope, peace, justice, and so on, is presumably one for which believers should yearn and towards which they should earnestly work.

One possible ethical implication that might follow from such a reading is indeed that there is no point in any Christian vocation to care for and preserve the earth, since it will eventually be renewed and recreated. It deserves to be said, however, that this is not necessarily the implication to be drawn. As Adams points out, none of the New Testament writers sees their expectation of coming cosmic catastrophe as reason to devalue the current material world or to desist from ethical and upright living (Adams 2007: 258–59). Indeed, Bouma-Prediger insists that "[i]t is a non sequitur to argue that because the earth will be destroyed in the future, humans, therefore, should exploit it in the present. To use an analogy, is it permissible for me to plunder your house just because some time in the future it will be torn down?" (Bouma-Prediger 2001: 78). Or as Douglas Moo suggests, using the analogy of the individual's body and the hope of resurrection: "I may believe that the body I now have is destined for radical transformation; but I am not for that reason unconcerned about what I eat or how much I exercise" (Moo 2006: 484). Nonetheless, if earth is to be destroyed, or the body resurrected, or a house torn down, then it is hard to find in these beliefs any significant or positive *motivation* or reason to care for and preserve the earth (or body, or house). To pursue Bouma-Prediger's analogy, if a house really does have an imminent demolition order, the owners are unlikely to repaint the bedrooms or refit the kitchen.

Given these and other difficulties, it is understandable that many ecological writers have taken a second approach, arguing that texts such as those we have surveyed in this (and the previous) chapter do not depict a final destruction of the earth but rather its renewal. As we have seen, this is a common strategy among those who argue that the Bible can be a source of positive ecological wisdom and provide the basis for an environmental ethic. However, there are major difficulties with this approach. For a start, it does not deal adequately with the content and likely meaning of the key texts. Bouma-Prediger's treatment of 2 Peter 3, for example, deals only with the textual point concerning whether the earth will be burnt or "found", and does not begin to consider all the other places in the text where the imagery of cosmic destruction is presented. Adams' thorough and historically informed analysis raises very serious doubts about whether one can plausibly deny that real cosmic collapse is what is envisaged in this and other New Testament texts. Moreover, as I have already stressed, even to conclude that what we have is a picture of renewal not of destruction – often presented as the crucial conclusion to support an ecological reading – does not resolve the difficulties. For the transformation in view is so radical and complete that it does not seem to matter how bad the previous state of the world had become, and anyway is something achieved by God, who turns the world into something very far removed from the functioning world as we know it.

A third approach, which Adams also hints at, is to acknowledge that the Bible contains different eschatological perspectives, rather than one consistent vision. Adams argues that alongside the vision of "unmaking and remaking" found in the cosmic catastrophe texts, there is "another strand … represented above all by Rom. 8:18–25 … that envisions the cosmic future in a different way … This passage seems to anticipate a non-destructive (yet radical) transformation of the existing creation" (Adams 2007: 256). Here, in contrast, say, to Revelation 21–22, "the redemptive activity itself is conceived differently: as an act of transformation rather than de-creation and re-creation" (p. 257). As I shall show in Part III of this book, I think it important to acknowledge the diversity of biblical material and to articulate reasons why certain texts and traditions might be prioritized and favoured over others. From the perspective of an ecological theology, there may indeed be good grounds to place Romans 8 centre stage – as indeed many ecotheologies have done (see ch. 7 above). But, as indicated above (and already in ch. 7, pp. 78–80), this does not by any means suffice to resolve the difficulties: even the radical transformation of Romans 8 leaves issues to be considered about what role (if any) humans might have in the process of liberating creation and what (if any) environmental ethical responsibilities this might imply.

It seems, then, that the biblical texts leave us with an uncertain and ambivalent legacy when it comes to the possible contribution of their future visions to theological and ethical views of the environment. None of the three strategies outlined above deals adequately with the difficulties, nor provides robust reason not to follow what an increasing majority find to be an unacceptable position: that the exploitation of earth should simply continue apace in view of God's imminent rescue. This is something of the interpretative challenge to which I now turn, in the final section of this book.

Further reading

Wright, N. T., *New Heavens, New Earth: the Biblical Picture of Christian Hope* (Cambridge: Grove, 1999).

Adams, Edward, *The Stars Will Fall From Heaven: Cosmic Catastrophe in the New Testament and its World* (Library of New Testament Studies 347; London and New York: T. & T. Clark, 2007).

Dyer, Keith D. (2002), "When Is the End Not the End? The Fate of Earth in Biblical Eschatology (Mark 13)", in Norman C. Habel and Vicky Balabanski (eds), *The Earth Story in the New Testament* (EB 5; Sheffield: Sheffield Academic Press), 44–56.

Finger, Thomas (1998), *Evangelicals, Eschatology, and the Environment* (The Scholars Circle; Wynnewood, PA: Evangelical Environmental Network).

Lucas, Ernest (1999), "The New Testament Teaching on the Environment", *Transformation*, 16:3: 93–99 (reprinted in Sam Berry *et al.*, *A Christian Approach to the Environment*, The John Ray Initiative, 2005).

Moo, Douglas J. (2006), "Nature in the New Creation: New Testament Eschatology and the Environment", *Journal of the Evangelical Theological Society* 49: 449–88.

Part III

Dealing with an Ambivalent Legacy: Proposals for an Ecological Hermeneutic

Chapter 10

Towards an Ecological Hermeneutic: Biblical Texts and Doctrinal Lenses

In the preceding survey of biblical texts and their various interpretations, one prominent result is, in a sense, a negative one: the Bible, I have argued, is ambivalent and ambiguous in terms of its ecological implications. Some texts are problematic for an ecological perspective, notably those that present humankind as rulers over the earth, or depict (and eagerly anticipate) a future cosmic collapse; while others offer an apparently more positive ecological contribution, notably those which relativize the importance of humanity and stress the inclusion of all creation in God's saving purposes. But even these latter texts, favourites among ecotheologians, are more ambivalent and uncertain in their theological and ethical implications than is often presumed. This finding raises difficult questions about the role and contribution of the Bible in shaping Christian thinking about the environment and human responsibility towards it. And however much interpreters argue for a certain reading as the correct one, it is clear enough from the material we have surveyed that the biblical texts can be read and construed in a wide variety of ways.

This ambivalence of the material and competing array of interpretations does not apply only to issues of ecology. It is interesting to compare, for example, the competing biblical interpretations related to the issues of slavery and women's rights. In the slavery debates of nineteenth century North America, exegetes argued both for abolitionist and anti-abolitionist positions, finding support in the Bible, sometimes from different texts, sometimes from the same texts (see Swartley 1983; Meeks 1996). Similarly, more recent arguments about women's equality and leadership roles have focused on competing interpretations of crucial biblical texts, notably those in the Pauline letters (Gal. 3:28; 1 Cor. 11:2–16; 14:34–35; 1 Tim. 2:9–15, etc.).

Despite the fact that much exegetical energy is expended on attempts to demonstrate the correct – or at least the most plausible – way to understand a given text, we have to face the fact that the biblical texts are open to a range of readings and have, indeed, been read in a variety of ways through Christian history. More disturbing, perhaps, is the further possibility that the most plausible reading of the texts, assuming there to be one, may support the ethical stance we find least acceptable. Wayne Meeks, for example, argues that the pro-slavery advocates had the more persuasive exegesis on their side, even though most would now agree in finding the institution of slavery morally repugnant (Meeks 1996). The same might be said, arguably at least, in regard to women's equality, gay rights, and environmental care. What should interpreters do if the Bible cannot – despite many claims to the contrary – provide an objective, clear perspective distinct from the interests and convictions of each particular interpreter, and if the biblical perspective may in fact, at least in certain texts, run counter to what we sense is the *right* moral stance?

As we seek to explore an answer to these dilemmas, and progress towards a more positive engagement with the biblical material, it is first worth returning to the diverse approaches to engaging the Bible in relation to ecological issues, outlined in Part I (ch. 2) above. The survey of texts and interpretations in Part II of the book should have helped to make clear some of the difficulties with these approaches, especially the approach I labelled "recovery". Most prominent in ecological writing about the Bible, this approach essentially aims to show that the Bible supports and promotes an attitude of care for creation; it has positive things to say about the value of the whole of creation and the associated human ethical responsibilities. This involves both a focus on (sometimes neglected) texts which seem to offer positive resources in this regard (e.g. Job 38–41) and an attempt to show that apparently problematic texts (such as Gen. 1:26–28 and 2 Pet. 3:10–13) are not as problematic as sometimes thought.

There are several problems that emerge. One is that the problematic texts cannot be so easily dealt with. As we have seen, it is difficult to deny that Gen. 1:26–28 is at least open to a plausible reading in which it is seen to place humanity in a unique position of sovereignty and dominion over creation. And texts like 2 Peter 3 do seem to envisage an impending collapse of the cosmos. Apologetic attempts to evade such conclusions are finally unconvincing. And even if eschatological texts assume some sense of continuity between old and new creation, the transformation (by God) is so radical that it is questionable whether this gives any clear basis or motivation for caring for the "old" creation. A second problem is that even the apparently most valuable eco-texts do not straightforwardly imply any particular pattern of ethical responsibility towards creation. For a start, they invariably (and unavoidably) reflect their ancient context, with its particular cosmological and mythological presuppositions and its human priorities, for example related to the demands of a subsistence-level agricultural society. Modern science and a global economy give us a very different perspective on the world. Moreover, these texts do not draw out any environmental-ethical exhortations; for example, Paul does not urge the Christians at Rome to engage in any action which, directly at least, is intended to hasten and achieve the liberation of creation. A third problem is that what a "recovered" biblical environmental theology really seems to involve is not simply attending to all that the Bible says, but a prioritizing of certain texts and images, interpreted in a certain way, as in the approach which focuses on the theme of stewardship to encapsulate human responsibility towards the earth.

Indeed, a very different kind of (anti-)ecological reading of the Bible is possible, a reading I described above (ch. 2) as a kind of resistance – resistance to the contemporary ecological agenda. For some readers, determined to give the Bible full authority and to resist the sway of contemporary cultural and ethical appeals, it seems clear that the Bible does give humanity sovereign dominion over the earth, and promises salvation for the elect and destruction for the wicked (and for the "old" earth). Despite the apologetic efforts of environmentally-minded evangelicals, it is difficult to deny that this perspective has some purchase, since certain texts can plausibly be read to support such a viewpoint. However, once again, these perspectives involve a clear prioritizing of certain biblical texts and images, interpreted in quite specific ways and systematized into a doctrinal scheme. Furthermore, I do not think this doctrinal stance can be shown to be wrong through biblical exegesis alone. The ambivalence of the texts and their openness to diverse interpretations means that various construals of "biblical teaching" are possible; though it is important to note that, despite the claims of those who present them, none of these is, or could ever be, simply a presentation of "what the Bible says". As Richard Hays puts it:

> "The Devil can cite Scripture to his purpose," so my grandmother used to say. Or, as we prefer to say now in the academy, "The text has inexhaustible hermeneutical potential" … the Bible itself contains diverse points of view, and diverse interpretive methods can yield diverse readings of any given text. (Hays 1997: 1)

What all this means, in effect, is that a response to our ecological crises cannot be derived just from reading the Bible carefully and attentively – though I would want to maintain that this is an important task. In the language of philosophical discourse, such careful reading is a *necessary* but not a *sufficient* condition for the development of an ecological theology and ethics. We cannot simply ask "what does the Bible say" about this topic. Just as "what the Bible says" about slavery and women is varied, complex, and (in parts) morally objectionable, so is what it "says" about the environment. We cannot "follow the maker's instructions" by reading and obeying the Bible on this or any other subject of theological or ethical importance (cf. Rogerson 2007:1–7). It makes no sense to claim that Scripture alone is "sufficient" in such matters, and that the task of Christian theology and ethics is simply to collect and understand "all the relevant passages in the Bible on various topics and then summaris[e] their teachings clearly so that we know what to believe" (Grudem 1994: 21; cf. 26, 127–34).

An alternative approach is that taken by the Earth Bible project, in which there is a clear recognition that what the biblical texts say is varied, and that some texts may be objectionable and problematic from an ecojustice perspective. This approach therefore insists that (some) biblical texts must be resisted, while others are more open to ecological retrieval; suspicion and recovery belong together in the interpretative task. I agree that this more nuanced and critical approach to biblical interpretation is preferable and, at the end of the day, more honest, since it does not require, say, that the environmentally committed Christian must try to show that 2 Peter 3 does not really imply the destruction of the cosmos. She can concede that this is what the text means, but then give reasons for rejecting what the text teaches, or at least for rejecting what some might take to be its implications. This implies, of course, a very different understanding of biblical authority. The method adopted by the Earth Bible Team, outlined above, involves commitment to a set of ecojustice principles (see pp. 13–14 above), which in effect encapsulate the theoretical and ethical convictions of the project. There is no claim that the Bible teaches, or necessarily even contains, these principles.

There is a major difficulty with this approach, however, at least in terms of an approach to doing Christian theology – an important qualification, since "doing Christian theology" is not necessarily any part of the project's aim. This is that authority effectively lies not with the Bible or the Christian tradition but with the ecojustice principles; it is these that present a set of norms to inspire and instruct human belief and action. These may well prove an attractive agenda to those already committed to the ecojustice cause. But the question is this: Why then should Christians find these principles *persuasive*, persuasive enough to serve as a basis for ethical commitment and critical evaluation of the Bible? (And who else should be particularly bothered about what the Christian Bible has to say about contemporary ecological commitment?) From where do these principles derive? Do they represent a specifically Christian theology and ethics, a rearticulation of the Christian tradition? It is evident that the Team does *not* want to present the principles in this way, since they are described as having been developed "in dialogue with ecologists" but deliberately not formulated using biblical or theological terms, so as "to facilitate dialogue with biologists, ecologists, other religious traditions ... and scientists" (Earth Bible Team 2000: 38). Thus the principles seem to represent a encapsulation of modern, scientifically informed, ecological commitment, something formed *independently* of the Christian and biblical traditions, in which case the Bible is pretty much dispensable. Francis Watson, interestingly, traces this type of modern approach back to Immanuel Kant's attempt, in *Religion within the Limits of Reason Alone* (1793), to offer a philosophical account of how the truths embodied in biblical and Christian doctrine can be independently discerned by "reason". Watson comments:

> Kant's work is the forerunner of all more recent attempts to interpret scripture on the basis of an ethical-political criterion that is already known independently of the texts. Scripture can only say what the criterion allows it to say [or, we might add, is criticised and resisted where it does not say this], and what it is allowed to say is only what we can already say to ourselves even without scripture. The textual embodiment of the criterion is of only limited usefulness, for the particularity of biblical narrative is an imperfect and potentially misleading vehicle for the universal truths of reason or for the various contemporary projects of liberation. (Watson 2008, in press)

Watson's point, it seems to me, is to insist that this cannot be an adequate approach to the role of the Bible in Christian theology – it reflects far too weak a doctrine of Scripture – since it does not give the Bible a generative and normative role in the ongoing articulation and reformulation of Christian doctrine.

A way forward? Doctrinal lenses and the process of interpretation

How then might we find and articulate a way between the alternatives outlined above? Here I turn to the approach to biblical interpretation outlined by Ernst Conradie (see Conradie 2008; forthcoming). Conradie outlines a number of factors that influence interpretation of the Bible: first, there is the text in its original historical context; then there are the various traditions of interpretation through the ages; there is the contemporary context that shapes the questions and issues readers bring to the text; and there is a wide range of hidden interests that have shaped the text and its interpretation from its time of production to the present day. Meaning is made in the ongoing encounter – a "spiral of ongoing interpretation" – between reader and text, an encounter shaped by all the factors listed above. What this suggests is that the interpretation of the Bible is a constructive act, shaped and influenced by the text, by the modern context, and by the various traditions of reading and interpreting represented in (and beyond) Christian theology.

According to Conradie, it is important to appreciate how appropriation of the Bible in Christian theology is shaped by heuristic or doctrinal keys, central ideas or motifs which give fundamental shape to a theological tradition. These doctrinal keys "are not directly derived from either the Biblical texts or the contemporary world but are precisely the product of previous attempts to construct a relationship between text, tradition and context" (Conradie 2006: 306). They are *made* in the ongoing encounter between reader and text, and in the attempt to fuse the distant horizons of both. These doctrinal constructs, as Conradie labels them in a recent essay, have a triple function:

> They provide a strategy to identify *both* the meaning of the contemporary context *and* of the biblical texts. They therefore (and simultaneously) enable the interpreter also to establish a *link* between text and contemporary context. Doctrinal constructs are not only employed to *find* similarities but to *construct* similarities, to *make* things similar, if necessary. The scope of such doctrinal constructs is often quite comprehensive: they purport to provide a clue to the core meaning of the contemporary context *as a whole* and the Biblical text *as a whole*. (Conradie 2009: 201)

It may perhaps be valuable to imagine these doctrinal constructs as something like a two-way lens, which shapes and focuses the biblical traditions – bringing certain themes into clear and central focus, blurring, distorting, or marginalizing others – and at the same time both reflects and shapes our understanding of, and response to, the contemporary context. Just as any lens offers a positive new way to construct relevant meaning from the Bible, so also, Conradie insists, it will inevitably "distort" both text and context, perhaps ideologically – that is, in legitimating and concealing the interests of dominant social groups. Doctrinal lenses should thus be subject to a hermeneutic of suspicion (Conradie 2006: 308); we must ask critical questions about the plausibility and the impact of all such constructions. What do they make us see, from whose perspective, and how do they skew it? But precisely one of the advantages of identifying these doctrinal constructs explicitly is that it makes clear that we are not simply claiming to read or present what the text "says", but are acknowledging that our reading of the Bible is a *construction,* shaped by certain priorities and convictions.

Before we turn to the specific application of this approach to the ecological reading of the Bible, it may be helpful to consider one or two other examples which illustrate something of how this approach illuminates the history of biblical and theological interpretation (cf. also Conradie 2006: 306–09). Augustine (354–430 CE) insisted that the only valid understanding of the scriptures is that which serves to build up the love of God and love of neighbour, seeing the central message of the Bible as encapsulated in the summary Jesus gave as the heart of the commandments (Mark 12:28–34 and parallels). Augustine wrote: "anyone who thinks that he has understood the divine scriptures or any part of them, but cannot by his understanding build up this double love of God and neighbour, has not yet succeeded in understanding them" (*On Christian Doctrine,* 1:35–40). Similarly, "when someone has learnt that the aim of the commandment is 'love from a pure heart, and good conscience and genuine faith' [1 Tim. 1:5], he will be ready to relate every interpretation of the holy scriptures to these three things and may approach the task of handling these books with confidence" (1:40–44). Augustine saw the central teaching of the Bible to be summarized in the command to love God and neighbour, and therefore saw this as a guiding principle for interpretation; anyone who read the Bible in a way which was not shaped by this central lens and did not support this teaching had misunderstood what the scriptures were all about.

A still clearer example of the role of doctrinal constructs in biblical interpretation may be found in the tradition associated with the great Protestant reformer, Martin Luther (1483–1546). Luther was reading the Bible in a specific socio-religious context – as a monk under the disciplines of the Catholic Church, in which forgiveness for sins had become tied up with a demanding process of penance and payment of indulgences. Luther found in the scriptures, specifically in Paul's letters to the Romans and the Galatians, a doctrine which he came to see as central to the Christian gospel: justification by faith. Not only was this doctrine developed from careful exegesis of the crucial Pauline texts, but it also came to serve as a dominant lens with which then to read the Bible.

Once justification by faith became established as the central doctrinal focus for Luther and the Lutheran tradition, the corollary was a critical stance towards any texts which might appear to teach justification by works or which did not clearly point to Jesus Christ. Luther was famously negative about the letter of James, regarding it as an "epistle of straw", because it says nothing about the death and resurrection of Christ and appears to teach justification by works (Jas 2:1–26; Chester and Martin 1994: 3). James thus became a rather marginal and neglected text, compared with the theologically crucial Pauline letters. Interpreters in the Lutheran tradition have generally continued this focus on the key Pauline letters, Romans and Galatians above all, and have continued to defend the idea that justification by faith is both exegetically and theologically crucial.

An interesting comparison – with some notable contrasts – may be found in the much more recent movement known as Liberation Theology. Beginning in the early 1970s with seminal works such as Gustavo Gutiérrez's *A Theology of Liberation* (1974 [1971]), this movement, rooted in the experience of the churches in Latin America, was driven to a new reading of the Bible by the pressing demands of a particular socio-political context, one of grinding poverty and violent oppression (see Boff and Boff 1987). In biblical stories such as the Exodus, where God rescues the enslaved people of Israel from oppression in Egypt, theologians reading the Bible in a context of poverty and oppression found a key motif: God as liberator of the poor. Other texts, such as Luke 4:16–21, where Jesus proclaims that his message is to bring "good news to the poor … to let the oppressed go free …", are also of central importance. Interestingly, from the perspective of liberation, Paul is a much more ambivalent figure, who may be suspected of having hindered the cause of freedom with his instructions to slaves and wives to be submissive (cf., e.g., 1 Cor. 7:17–24; 11:3–10; 14:34–35; Col. 3:18–4.1; 1 Tim. 2:9–15). Paul's letters, then, have been comparatively neglected by those seeking a liberating message from the Bible. But the letter of James, with its harsh critique of the rich and powerful and its message of hope for the poor (e.g. Jas 1:9–10; 2:1–8; 5:1–8), has been rediscovered as a crucial canonical voice (cf. Chester and Martin 1994: 54–60). One thing this shows is the way in which the value and pertinence of texts, and their ability to challenge and discomfort us, changes with time and context. As Conradie stresses, interpretation happens in the interaction between the reader's contemporary context and the ancient text, so changing contexts and demands bring new perspectives and doctrines to light.

One of the benefits of understanding the process of interpretation in this way is that it gives a more honest insight into what theological and ethical engagement with the Bible involves. As we return to the specific issues of ecology, an example from this field may be helpful. As we have already seen (pp. 28–30), stewardship has become a central idea in much environmental theology, especially that from an evangelical perspective. Stewardship is often presented as what the Bible teaches. According to Wesley Granberg-Michaelson, for example, rather than giving "humankind permission to take the earth into their own hands and use it to suit their selfish purposes ... the Bible sees the nature of humanity's dominion as service for the sake of all creation" (Granberg-Michaelson 1987a: 3; cf. also Wilkinson *et al.* 1980: 203–38; Dyrness 1987). But it should by now be clear that there are major difficulties in any claim that "the Bible teaches" that stewardship is the correct and divinely commanded character of humanity's relationship to creation, not to mention questions about whether stewardship is such a sound basis for human relationship to the rest of creation as its proponents suggest (see pp. 29–30 above).

It is, however, entirely plausible to see stewardship as one kind of doctrinal lens that might inform and shape an ecological theology. It can be derived from a certain kind of reading of particular biblical texts, and it can be *placed* centre-stage, like the themes of justification by faith or liberation, such that it shapes ongoing engagement with the Bible. Yet it is crucially important to identify it as a doctrinal lens or construct, rather than what the Bible simply "says", because there is then an honesty about the extent to which this is an interpretative construction, which invites critical reflection rather than unquestioned acceptance. And indeed, some would criticize its ethical and theological value (see esp. Palmer 1992).

What then would this more nuanced and hermeneutically-explicit approach to engaging the Bible with questions of ecology look like? There are three dimensions to the task that need to be brought together. First, there is an important role for *historical study and informed exegesis*. This helps to ensure that we attend carefully to the content of the biblical texts, and do not too easily forget that they are products of an ancient culture, in which assumptions and concerns were very different from our own. Second, there is a need for interpretation to be informed by the *theological tradition*. This claim does not apply, of course, to every kind of engagement with the Bible, some of which are rigorously historical or archaeological, others of which are driven by contemporary concerns outside the domain of Christian theology. But an approach which is concerned to engage afresh with the Bible, in order to consider how Christian theology and ethics may be reshaped and rearticulated in the light of contemporary issues and demands, must do so in dialogue with the Christian tradition(s), steering a difficult but necessary course between conservative preservation of that tradition and radical alteration of it. The kind of approach needed to bring that tradition to address new issues such as our contemporary ecological problems may be labelled one of "re-formation" – taking the word in its etymological sense. This is well captured by Paul Santmire, who describes this approach as one taken by those he calls "revisionists", who stand somewhere between conservative apologists and radical reconstructionists:

> Since ... the Old and New Testaments are the font of the classical theological tradition in the West, and since these scriptures are taken as the chief norm for all teachers and teachings (*norma normans*) by the tradition itself, the revisionists, as a matter of course, also have given the highest priority to biblical interpretation. At the same time, however, the dynamics of the classical tradition, thus understood, constantly call forth a *re-forming* of the tradition itself, as that term itself has historically suggested. (Santmire 2000: 7–8)

A third dimension to the task is an engagement with *contemporary science* and other fields of human knowledge (such as ethics) relevant to understanding the ecological issues that confront us. This, of course, is also a controversial claim, for some would insist that Christians must accept what the Bible teaches, even where this flatly contradicts the picture that emerges through modern scientific study. Without being able here to defend the claim in full, I would argue for an approach that sees (not uncritically!) truth and insight in various fields of scholarship, in other religions and cultural traditions; that is, for a model of theology as engaged in dialogue with, not isolated from, other disciplines and realms of human knowledge. This means that advances in science, and also in ethics and in our sense of the moral status of both humans and animals, should shape and inform a critical reading of the biblical tradition. Liberation theology, for example, has drawn (controversially, for some) not only on the biblical and theological tradition, but also on analysis of the contemporary social and political situation offered by social science, and by Marxist analysis in particular. Similarly, an ecological theology and ethics must be informed, but not dictated, by the analyses of our world's ecosystems, climate, future trajectories, and so on, offered by the range of contemporary natural sciences.

Overall, the kind of approach outlined by Conradie would, it seems to me, invite an engagement with the biblical texts that is exegetically serious – otherwise it ceases to be a genuine attempt at reading – but which also acknowledges such an engagement to be, inevitably, a constructive and creative act, shaped by the perceived priorities of the contemporary context, and informed in that perception by science, and all the means of insight available to us. As such, these readings will be provisional, corrigible, open to critical suspicion and ongoing reformulation. To function as a form of constructive Christian theological engagement does not imply that such a reading must avoid any criticism of biblical texts. But it does mean that there will be some positive construction of doctrinal lenses, formed in the encounter between reader and text, which in turn may serve as a basis for critical appropriation. This will entail an attempt to (re)read the tradition from a particular perspective, one which, *on theological and ethical grounds*, discerns where and how the word of "good news" is to be found. Just as Luther found in Paul a message of justification by faith, through grace alone, which then became the hermeneutical and theological heart of the Lutheran tradition, shaping a whole tradition of (critical) biblical interpretation and theological doctrine, so our own context, with its ecological crises and environmental pressures, may inspire new kinds of engagement with the Bible, new readings with new doctrinal lenses at their heart. It remains, in the final chapter, to offer some preliminary sketch of what that new reading might look like.

Further reading

Jasper, David, *A Short Introduction to Hermeneutics* (Louisville, KY: Westminster John Knox, 2004)

Kelsey, David H., *The Uses of Scripture in Recent Theology* (London; SCM, 1975).

Conradie, Ernst M., "Towards an Ecological Biblical Hermeneutics: A Review Essay on the Earth Bible Project", *Scriptura* 85 (2004) 123–35.

———, "The Road Towards an Ecological Biblical and Theological Hermeneutics", *Scriptura* 93 (2006) 305–14.

———, "Interpreting the Bible amidst Ecological Degradation", *Theology* 112 (2009) 199–207.

———, "What on Earth is an Ecological Hermeneutics? Some Broad Parameters", in David G. Horrell, Cherryl Hunt, Christopher Southgate and Francesca Stavrakopoulou (eds), *Ecological Hermeneutics: Biblical, Historical, and Theological Perspectives* (London and New York: T. & T. Clark, forthcoming).

Horrell, David G., Hunt, Cherryl and Southgate, Christopher, "Appeals to the Bible in Ecotheology and Environmental Ethics: A Typology of Hermeneutical Stances", *Studies in Christian Ethics* 21 (2008) 219–38.

Chapter 11

A Critical Ecological Biblical Theology and Ethics

In this final chapter, I offer some tentative proposals concerning ways in which a creative and constructive engagement with the biblical texts might proceed, following the kind of approach outlined in the previous chapter. This involves consciously bringing certain texts and themes into central focus, marginalizing or resisting others. The image of the lens is helpful to envisage the process at work: when we shake a kaleidoscope the rearrangement of the pieces and the new refractions of light make a different image. Similarly, different shapes and configurations of glass make a view look different, and also change the appearance of the viewer's eye. Reading the Bible afresh in light of the environmental issues that face us involves reconfiguring the landscape, recasting the story, seeing the whole thing differently, and at the same time seeing ourselves and our world differently too. I should stress that this is, inevitably, a brief and sketchy outline which may perhaps help to stimulate and provoke more detailed and systematic work along similar lines. In the first part of the chapter, I outline some theological foundations; in the second part, I turn to ethical implications.

Theological foundations

In the previous chapter I outlined an approach to biblical interpretation which, following Ernst Conradie, avoids, on the one hand, the claim to be presenting simply what the Bible says, and on the other hand, measuring the Bible critically against a pre-determined and non-biblical canon of modern values. It operates instead with the notion of doctrinal lenses, which arise from a reading of the text shaped by the context and concerns of the reader and then shape and inform further reading and theological reflection. Below, then, are some of the main ideas that have emerged from our survey of biblical texts in Part II, and which might stand as doctrinal lenses at the heart of an ecological theology. These may function to reorient a theological appropriation of the biblical traditions, just as central motifs such as "justification by faith" and "liberation" have done when readers have faced particular challenges in the world. The varying length of the sections below, it should be noted, does not by any means reflect their relative importance in such a theological reorientation.

The goodness of all creation

One of the repeated refrains in the influential story of creation with which the Christian and Jewish Bible opens is that God declares everything "good" (see ch. 3 above). In its original context, as we noted above, this may not imply moral perfection, but perhaps something more like "fit for purpose" (so Rogerson 1991: 60–61); it is "very good" (Gen. 1:31) insofar as its ordered harmony, as a whole, sustains and enables life. But even in this sense the assertion stands as an indication that the created world is valuable and beautiful in its ordered functioning, and is certainly not, as some early Christian "heretics" suggested, to be regarded as evil matter, the product of some lesser deity. This declaration of the goodness of all creation is, then, a simple but profoundly important affirmation, which has (too) often required reassertion in the face of frequent tendencies in the Christian tradition to denigrate the material world. Francis Watson, for example, shows how Irenaeus affirms the goodness of creation in his second-century arguments with the Gnostics (Watson forthcoming); in our day this may continue to need reassertion in the face of a focus on the part of some Christians on the value of the "spiritual" dimensions of life and the (supposed) salvation and survival (only) of the "soul". Sectarian tendencies within and since the biblical tradition have sometimes served to generate theologies which stress the contrast between the goodness of the holy elect and the wickedness of the fallen world. While these too have their value in certain contexts – for example when the Church is in danger of accommodating too closely to the established powers and structures of the world – their potentially negative implications for human attitudes to the earth need to be resisted. Indeed, careful re-reading of biblical texts in light of ecological questions can show how material and spiritual are presented as inseparable, and God and the world as intrinsically connected. For example, in a study of the Hebrew word *ruach* (meaning spirit/Spirit, air, breath, wind, etc.), Theodore Hiebert shows how its material and spiritual, worldly and Godly dimensions are bound up inseparably together; the distinctions drawn between matter and spirit, body and soul, are more the product of Western dualism influencing interpreters than of the text itself (Hiebert 2008). Such readings can therefore help to challenge the influential spiritual/material dualism, which, like other dualisms of the Western tradition, has been exposed as problematic in its assumptions and implications, not least in terms of human attitudes towards the environment. At the centre of this re-reading of the biblical tradition, which offers the basis for a holistic sense of the interconnectedness of human and non-human creation, of God and world, of spiritual and material, stands the emphatic declaration of Gen. 1:31, that "God saw everything that he had made, and behold, it was very good" (ESV). Our sense of what that term "good" implies may well have developed from that which the original writers envisaged, given changing contexts and challenges, and developing insights into the functioning of the world of nature. But such is the nature of biblical interpretation, as we have seen through this book; our sense of creation's goodness is informed, now, not only by the biblical texts but by contemporary science and ethics, and specifically by ecology. The goodness of all creation is a fundamental principle that implies something like the Earth Bible Team's ecojustice principle of the "intrinsic worth" of all things (see p. 13 above) and should underpin any ecological theological and ethical reflection.

Humanity as part of the community of creation
The declaration of Gen. 1:26–28 that humanity was "made in the image of God" and given dominion over the earth has, for understandable reasons, been a prominent focus for the construction of doctrine, leading to a stress on the uniqueness and special value of humanity. Some sense of humanity's unique place in the created order, some degree of anthropocentrism, will likely remain a proper component of a Christian theology; radical rejection of all such tendencies can only be sustained in a very major departure from Christian orthodoxy. What is more important to explore, it seems to me, is what kind of anthropocentrism might legitimately be espoused. After all, it is undoubtedly the case that humanity has a unique ability to *reflect* on the current ecological issues facing the planet and to *act* in ways self-consciously formed by that reflection. That said, we should not overstate the extent of human influence and power, as Stephen Webb does when he asserts: "The world is shrinking and humans are in charge of all of it, for better or worse. We cannot shirk our responsibility for nature. Nature is largely under our control. The only question is how we will exercise that control" (Webb 2001: 24). While I sympathize with Webb's concern to nurture a sense of human responsibility for the non-human world, mere observation of nature should show how little "control" we humans exercise: floods and tsunamis, droughts and earthquakes, not to mention the broader picture of climate change, illustrate how little we have nature in our power,

even when natural events are caused by our actions. An anthropocentric theology should not be an occasion for the expression of human arrogance.

David Clough proposes a significant distinction between a kind of instrumental anthropocentrism, in which humans have a central place in the process by which God redeems the whole creation (as in Rom. 8:19–23), and a teleological anthropocentrism, in which humans have a central importance in the redeemed creation. Clough accepts that the former kind of anthropocentrism is indeed evident in the biblical texts but argues that the latter kind should be firmly rejected, and has no intrinsic or necessary place in Christian theology (Clough forthcoming).

Indeed, given the insights science is currently giving us, not only into the extent of the ecological impacts of human activity, but also into the extent to which we share much of our composition and characteristics with other species, there is a strong case to be made that what we now need to emphasize is the fact that humanity is but one element of a profoundly interconnected community of creation (again, an affirmation of one of the Earth Bible Team's ecojustice principles, that of interconnectedness). What is needed is a puncturing of human arrogance and sense of superiority more than an affirmation of our unique value. Such a reorientation might be resourced by the closing chapters of the book of Job, in which, as we have seen (ch. 5), God's speeches emphatically decentre humanity and depict God's relationship with all creation as existing entirely without regard for its relevance or benefit to humans. There are good theological and ethical grounds for bringing this kind of theology of creation to the centre, and for resisting and marginalizing, or at least significantly downplaying, texts which assert humanity's right to "dominate and subdue". Again, despite much Christian theology to the contrary, what we need to learn at the present time is not how unique or special we are to God, but how relatively unspecial we are, how much we share in common with other life forms on earth. New priorities call for new motifs to come centre stage.

Interconnectedness in failure and flourishing
One of the themes we have repeatedly seen, especially in texts from the Old Testament, is that of inextricable connection between the fate of humans, animals, plants and land. Whether this be in a negative way, as when human disobedience stands at the commencement of a story of general degradation and decay (see ch. 4), or in a positive way, as when prophets dream of a time of fertility and flourishing in a future time of righteousness (see ch. 8), the essential connections remain the same. Humanity's right relationship with God, sustained by obedience, by worship and right ritual,

and so on, is equally reflected in right relationships with the land, and vice versa. Indeed, in some biblical texts we have not explored, such as the book of Leviticus, the land may be seen as an important character, bound up like humans in covenant relationship with God, requiring its own sabbath rest, and vomiting out the people when they are disobedient (see Morgan 2009).

It was once perhaps easy to dismiss such ideas as reflections of a "primitive", pre-scientific worldview, in which unenlightened agriculturalists sought through religious ritual to ensure the right mix of sunshine and rain to bring forth good crops. But with our developing ecological awareness, such views acquire a new and timely, almost ominous, character. From a very different perspective, science too informs us of the extent to which actions and effects are intricately connected in the delicate ecosystems of which we are a part. Spraying pesticides to kill a troublesome parasite can have a knock-on effect on many other forms of wildlife, and on human health too, as Rachel Carson classically demonstrated (Carson 2000 [1962]). The idea that the land might vomit out its inhabitants is a powerful image, especially when juxtaposed with images of land that has become uninhabitable and uncultivatable due to overexploitation or climate change caused by human activity. This idea is again close to an Earth Bible ecojustice principle, that of the earth's *resistance* to injustice at the hands of humans. More positively, the images of future peace and plenty offer hope that a just pattern of relationships between humans, animals, plants and land, can lead to a sustainable situation of mutual flourishing, though no one would be naively optimistic about the scale of the challenges that stand in the way. This particular biblical motif offers both challenge and contribution to a theology of sin that needs to move away from a classical focus on interpersonal relationships to a broader compass, to the whole network of (ecological) relationships in which the human animal is inextricably embedded. Right relationships and right actions – towards God and towards the earth – are bound up together in a vision of future flourishing.

The covenant with all creation
The story of the Flood, and of God's eternal covenant with which the story ends, offers a good example of the ways in which commentators' interests and presuppositions have shaped their reading of the text. As we have seen (ch. 4), the covenant has frequently been seen as a covenant with Noah and his descendants, with little attention given to the emphatic and repeated declarations in the text that this is a covenant with every living thing, with all the earth. Reread with an eye to this broader perspective, this account

presses us towards a less anthropocentric theology, away from a focus on humanity's special relationship with God and towards a sense that the whole creation is bound in covenant to God. Like the theme of the goodness of creation, the idea of God's covenant with all the earth can be briefly and simply stated. But its central importance should not be underemphasized. Here we have a further contribution to a doctrinal picture in which it is not merely the relationship between humans and God that is of concern, but where the relationship of the whole creation to God is at the centre.

Creation's calling to praise God

The relationship of the whole of creation to God also appears strongly in the theme of creation's praise (see ch. 5). As we noted there, it is not by any means straightforward to conceive this praise in ways that are scientifically cogent, theologically meaningful and ethically relevant. But there is, I think, a rich resource to be explored here. For a start, this theme helps once more to emphasize that the whole of creation, and not just humanity, is bound in covenant relationship with God and called into being to express praise of God. Scientific and theological language can legitimately stand side-by-side here, each offering a different kind of insight. The sounds of crashing waves or rustling leaves can be scientifically explained through the insights of physics. But they can also be seen as sounds of wonder and beauty, sounds which can be regarded as an expression of nature's praise to its creator. The Earth Bible's principle of "voice" captures a somewhat similar idea, though without any explicit theological orientation.

As we saw in Chapter 5, Richard Bauckham proposes that the biblical picture is of creation praising God "just by being itself". With typically elegant expression, Karl Barth makes a similar point: "even the smallest creatures", he says, make their jubilant if inadequate response to the divine glory. "They do it along with us or without us. They do it also against us to shame us and instruct us. They do it because they cannot help doing it". Thus:

> when man accepts his destiny in Jesus Christ … he is only like a late-comer slipping shamefacedly into creation's choir in heaven and earth, which has never ceased its praise, but merely suffered and signed, as it still does, that in inconceivable folly and ingratitude its living centre man does not hear its voice, its response, its echoing of the divine glory, or rather hears it in a completely perverted way, and refuses to co-operate in the jubilation which surrounds him. (Barth 1957: 648)

Barth's depiction here also reminds us both of the "suffering and sighing" of creation – an echo of Rom. 8:19–23 – and of the human failure to praise, which the praise of "even the smallest creatures" puts to shame. In Luke 19:37–40, when the Pharisees urge Jesus to silence the crowds' acclamation of him, Jesus replies, "I tell you, if these were silent, the stones would shout out" (Luke 19:40, NRSV). This may be interpreted as a reference to the stones' taking up the cry of praise, both as praise and as protest against the silencing of human praise (see Horrell and Coad forthcoming). And insofar as human failings include the failure to relate to non-human creation in ways informed by justice and peace, this notion of creation's praise as rebuke might contribute to a notion of ecological sin: creation's cry of praise is at the same time a rebuke of humanity's acquisitive self-absorption.

The notion that creation praises God simply by being itself might also have some ethical relevance; clearly, it would attribute an intrinsic value, even beauty, to the non-human world which would imply the imperative to preserve and not diminish the richness and diversity of creation. But it is questionable whether the notion that creation praises simply by being itself is as helpful to an ecological theology as Bauckham suggests. For one thing, this leaves aside the issue of the suffering and pain that characterize – and have always characterized – the non-human as well as the human experience. Can creation's experience unambiguously be described as a voicing of praise, when it also groans and suffers (cf. Rom. 8:19–23; see Southgate 2008b)? An ecological doctrine of creation must also do justice to the profound ambiguities in non-human as well as human experience. In ethical terms too, the idea that the human challenge is "to allow creation's praise by letting it be" (Bauckham 2002b: 52) is of some – but limited – value. Certainly it adds a theological underpinning to calls to preserve areas of wilderness, species, habitats, and so on. It may be valuable to cite a principle of "letting creation be" when it comes to decisions about whether to develop and exploit, or leave and preserve, specific areas of land. Yet many of the landscapes and species we see around us are already the product of the interaction between human and non-human creation, including those we now regard as of great beauty. Human beings are already bound up with the being of other species and communities, and we cannot now decide to simply "let them be".

An alternative way to conceptualize the notion of creation's praise is to view it as creation's calling, its goal and purpose (cf. Coad 2009). This is not necessarily to reject the notion that creation already praises God, but to give it a future and as yet incompletely fulfilled vocation – a notion which finds a parallel in the Earth Bible's ecojustice principle of purpose. Just as human praise is inadequate and partial, marred by suffering and sin, so too creation's praise is a mixture of joy and pathos from a groaning and polluted yet profoundly beautiful and wondrous world. On this view, both human and non-human praise strain forwards, anticipating an eschatological consummation in which the ambiguities of suffering will be no more. And this view too has ethical relevance, for it would imply that the challenge is to foster and promote both human and non-human praise. In relation to humans, we have long given attention, albeit still inadequately, to the kind of things that are necessary for human flourishing, for enabling humans to express joy and praise: access to adequate water, food and shelter; freedom from fear and violence; education and opportunity, and so on. In the case of non-human creation, while there are no easy or obvious ethical imperatives that can be "read-off" from the notion of creation's praise, there would seem to be a human imperative actively to foster beauty and richness of life, diversity and sustainable balance, such that the intricate web of life can continue to reflect and to voice its creator's glory. This would still imply an anthropocentric theology, in the sense that it gives humanity a central role, and a central responsibility, in the task of enabling both human and non-human praise. But this is a positively anthropocentric theology (and, in Clough's terms, an instrumental rather than teleological one) – one which retains a strong sense of human responsibility at the same time as stressing humanity's collaborative membership of what Barth calls "creation's choir".

Attention to this theme could also serve to reorientate the focus of classical Christian theology. For example, the famous Westminster Catechism of 1647, produced by the Westminster Assembly, established by Parliament in 1643 to reform the English Church, poses and answers its first doctrinal question thus: "What is the chief and highest end of man? Man's chief and highest end is to glorify God, and fully to enjoy him forever." Decades of feminist criticism have taught us that such language is gender exclusive, reflecting and reinscribing male dominance, so we might hastily reformulate the answer thus: "Humanity's chief and highest end is to glorify God, and fully to enjoy God forever." Our ecological reflections, informed by the theme of creation's praise in the Psalms and elsewhere, would suggest a further, equally radical, reformulation: "Creation's chief and highest end is to glorify God, and fully to enjoy God forever." Such a shift in doctrinal formulation would help to indicate that the hope and vocation of salvation are not only a matter for humans but for the whole created order.

Liberation and reconciliation for all things
Just as the conclusion to the Flood story records an eternal covenant made with all the earth, so the Pauline epistles, most notably in Rom. 8:19–23

and Col. 1:15–20, declare that the whole of creation is bound up in the redemption which God is bringing about in Christ (see ch. 7). In Romans 8, this is depicted as a liberation of creation from its bondage to decay, a liberation dependent on, and bound up with, the redemption of the (human) children of God, whose present suffering and groaning is echoed and paralleled by the whole creation and the holy Spirit. In Colossians 1, the universal redemption is described as an act of reconciliation, accomplished by God in Christ, through whom and to whom all things have been reconciled. These distinct but broadly coherent declarations are another important contribution to a theology which insists that the scope of God's creating, sustaining, and redeeming work is nothing less than all created things.

Doctrinal lenses for an ecological theology

These brief summaries of some of the biblical stories, themes, and motifs we have encountered in Part II of this study serve to indicate some of the potential doctrinal lenses which might stand at the centre of an ecological biblical theology and serve to reconfigure a reading of the whole. For example, while "justification by faith" as a central key has the problem of human sin and human salvation as its dominant topic, "the reconciliation of all things" recasts the doctrine of salvation in a way that takes its focus beyond human beings. Most of the themes mentioned above combine to move non-human creation from being merely the stage on which the drama of human redemption takes place to being fundamentally and inextricably bound up along with humans in this drama.

An ecological biblical theology might centre around a confession that God has created all things good, has bound Godself eternally in covenant to all the earth, calls all creation to a vocation of praise, and is bringing about the reconciliation and redemption of all things in Christ. Making these ideas the central lens through which we read and appropriate the Bible does not imply any pretence that this is simply what the Bible teaches, nor does it deny that there are plenty of other currents in the biblical tradition, some of which run contrary to the emphases encapsulated in our confession. But just as other doctrinal lenses and theological traditions have – sometimes without making this explicit – brought certain motifs and ideas to the centre, marginalizing or resisting others, so too a critical ecological biblical theology will entail a deliberate rearranging of what is central and what is marginal, what is to be reclaimed and what resisted, driven by what our contemporary context presses upon us as priorities. For example, while a certain anthropocentrism, understood in particular as a call to special responsibility, will likely remain embedded in an ecological Christian theology, texts which imply a human right to dominate and exploit the earth will be resisted and marginalized.

In the sections above, I have frequently noted that most of my biblical "theological foundations" bear a close comparison with one or other of the Earth Bible Team's ecojustice principles (see pp. 13–14). Indeed, Ernst Conradie has shown how the Earth Bible principles could be theologically reformulated as a "small dogmatics", a brief outline of Christian theology (Conradie 2006). Like the Earth Bible Team, I am convinced that the insights of science and our increasing awareness of the ecological problems we have caused should be taken on board and should result in a reorientation of our relationship to the earth. However, rather than derive a set of principles directly from dialogue with ecologists, scientists, members of other religions, and so on, and then use these critically to interrogate the biblical texts, I have sought to derive a series of ecological lenses from a reading of the biblical texts, though a reading which is also informed by scientific knowledge and contemporary understanding. This allows the Bible to play a more formative and foundational role in the constructive process of discerning principles, and thus can legitimately contribute to the reconfiguration of the Christian theological tradition. Indeed, while many of the emergent "principles" are broadly compatible with the Earth Bible's ecojustice principles, some aspects of an ecological biblical theology are likely to run somewhat counter to the Earth Bible approach – most notably in retaining a certain form of anthropocentrism, as opposed to the Earth Bible's general resistance to this. Moreover, some principles are differently conceived, because of the explicitly theological framework within which they are formulated: the Earth Bible's principle of voice, for example, is represented here by the notion of creation's praise of God.

There remains, however, one major difficulty we have encountered in the course of this study but which has not yet been addressed here: the problem of eschatology. Even if we focus on the future visions of transformation rather than those of destruction and replacement, there is still the question as to whether the promised future is so radically different from our present experience, and so dependent for its arrival on the sovereign action of God, that it effectively renders human environmental action ultimately pointless, and assures believers of a good and certain future whatever mess the planet ends up in. An attempt to address this important issue will follow, as we move to consider the ethical imperatives and implications that might flow from the kind of biblical theological foundations we have here outlined.

From theology to ethics, and the problem of eschatology

In outlining some of the central ideas which might resource an ecological biblical theology, it becomes clear that an eschatological vision is likely to be at the heart of the matter: it is the texts that depict some kind of future peace, a liberation for all creation, or announce the reconciliation of all things in Christ, that have understandably provided inspiration for ecological interpreters. And because eschatology is so central to the Christian reading of the biblical story, it remains unavoidably central to Christian theology and ethics. The coming of Christ has, from the earliest days, been seen as the beginning of the end, the decisive act of God to inaugurate the defeat of sin and death and bring to completion, eventually, the redemption of the world. When this eschatological hope is interpreted as a hope for a life after death in heaven, for a spiritual existence that lies beyond the material world, it can easily be taken to imply that environmental responsibility is an irrelevant preoccupation, focusing on the material at the expense of the spiritual, and distracting believers from their real priorities. Yet even when the hope is informed by those biblical texts that depict a renewal *of the earth*, and a *transformation* of the old creation into the new, there remain, as we have seen, questions about how far these visions inspire and motivate environmental care. If God will finally bring about the new creation, despite all the mess and wickedness in the world, and if this new creation is radically different from our current one – with no death, no predation, no suffering – then one might conclude that human actions to preserve the earth are somewhat irrelevant and, in the end, unnecessary.

There are, however, arguments to be made which can allow the eschatological visions of the biblical tradition positively to inform a Christian environmental ethics. The first point to stress is that the prophetic visions of a renewed, peaceable creation are often quite clearly intended to inspire and motivate conduct *in the present* (cf. e.g., Isa. 2:2–5; Mic. 4:1–5). A vision of the future functions to shape present conduct in line with that vision. In other words, visions of a glorious future are not intended to inculcate passivity, disengagement, or denigration of the material world (cf. Adams 2007).

A second important point is to emphasize that the earliest Christian eschatologies, as we glimpse them in the Gospels and in the letters of Paul, are *inaugurated* eschatologies. In other words, their shared conviction, expressed in different ways, is that the new creation, the kingdom of God, has already begun to be brought about, and is already visible in the here and now. This conviction strengthens still further the idea that the eschatological vision is meant to shape and inspire present action, and also implies that there has to be clear continuity between the present and whatever future will be finally brought about. The vision of the Synoptic Gospels, for example, is one in which Jesus' and his followers' acts of healing, acceptance, and table fellowship are indications of the presence of the kingdom of God (see ch. 6). The Gospel of John insists that eternal life begins here and now (John 5:24). For Paul, those who live in Christ have died to their old lives, to the old world, and now live in God's new creation, even though their current existence remains caught in the tension between the old and the new age (see ch. 7). And their conduct is meant to match their new identity in Christ. In other words, the shape of the hoped-for future is visible and enacted in the here and now, and implies a responsibility to act in ways congruent with that future, with participation in God's new creation. As Thomas Finger puts it, Christian environmental action "can be deeply eschatological in the sense that eschatological vision, combined with confidence in the eschaton's presence, provides the basic patterns and motivation for action" (Finger 1998: 31).

There remains, of course, the important question of what will actually follow in the future, what it is that Christians might hope God will bring about. Some believe that there will indeed be resurrection life beyond the grave for all who have lived, or at least all who have believed in Christ. There really will be a new creation, in which death is no more, even if it might be conceded that any insight into the character of this new creation will be fragmentary and partial, available only in images and metaphors (cf. 1 Cor. 13:9–12). Others will consider that the vision of a paradisiacal future, of life after death, of a peaceable non-predatory new creation, is precisely a vision, a dream, a hope, which can inspire and guide our action, but which need not, and probably will not, have any "real" fulfilment beyond this world as we know it. Moreover, just as Christians have had to think long and hard about how to reconcile the insights of the biblical creation stories with a scientific understanding of the world's origins, so too there is the challenge of integrating biblical visions of the future with the scenarios that science depicts, which would certainly suggest a massively long timescale before the present universe comes to any kind of physical end, whether in the heat death of a cosmic crunch, or the cold freeze of ongoing expansion (cf. Barton forthcoming). But it seems to me that, so far as the implications for environmental action go, either kind of conviction regarding the eschatological future visions – whether "realist" or "non-realist" – carries essentially the same implications. While the realist view probably carries greatest danger of disengagement from the present world, since it implies the conviction that God really will bring about something new, something "beyond the grave", as opposed to the non-realist view, in which the present earth is all we have, in both cases the measure of commitment and conviction concerning the eschatological vision is precisely and only seen in the extent to which it shapes and informs how people live now.

So the kind of theological foundations I have outlined above, and especially their (inaugurated) eschatological visions, can perhaps offer a basis for a reshaping of Christian theology, a renewed kind of worldview which will also have practical consequences in action (cf. also Finger 1998: 33–36). That is to say, in shaping what people do and decide, this renewed worldview offers resources for ethics as well as theology. What kind of ethical implications might there be, based on the kind of ecological biblical theology I have briefly sketched above?

We must start to explore that question at a somewhat general level, with the kind of broad implications and guiding principles that might emerge from the material I have highlighted. So, ethical action will, to begin with, be guided by convictions concerning the goodness of all creation, the interconnectedness of all creation, humanity included, and the calling of all creation to praise. Insofar as the eschatological visions shape ethical practice, then ethics will be shaped by the desire to work towards peace, reconciliation, and unity, not merely among humans, but among all created things. Some of these broad motifs come together, for example, in a conviction that the flourishing of humanity cannot be conceived, and certainly not achieved, except by regarding it as intrinsically bound up with the flourishing of the ecosystems in which humans are embedded, in the flourishing of the earth and its manifold species and forms of life. And insofar as this flourishing is seen as a fostering of the praise of all creation, it will probably also imply a concern for beauty – a somewhat nebulous and subjective concept, to be sure, but one which is essential to a sense of what the flourishing and praise of nature would include.

The central motifs of New Testament ethics also have an important contribution to offer to a biblical ecotheology and ethics, in suggesting a basic pattern of action through which peace and reconciliation are to be achieved. For Paul, for example, the central Christian obligation may be summed up as the imperative to imitate Christ in his self-giving for others; this "other-regard" is the means to achieve and sustain the unity and solidarity of the community (see Horrell 2005: 166–245; ch. 7 above). So, for example, Paul urges the Corinthian Christians to give money to the poor believers in Jerusalem, in imitation of the self-giving of Christ (2 Cor. 8:1–15), and appeals to the Philippian Christians to relate to one another in a way shaped by the pattern of Christ's self-emptying (Phil. 2:4–11). With some constructive rethinking in light of the ethical challenges that now face us, this pattern of Christ-like other-regard may be extended to inform actions and relationships not only beyond the Christian community but beyond the human community too (see Hunt 2009). In other words, just as Paul sees the unity and reconciliation of the early Christian communities as a goal dependent on the Christ-like self-giving of the members for one another, so we may see the reconciliation and flourishing of the community of living things on earth as dependent on the willingness of the powerful human species to consider the needs of other species – on whose wellbeing, ultimately, human wellbeing also depends – even in a costly, self-denying way (cf. Southgate 2008b: 101–03, who outlines an ecological form of "ethical kenosis", a self-emptying with regard to our aspirations, appetites, and acquisitiveness). Just as Paul assures the Corinthians that his aim in asking them to give is not that they might themselves experience poverty and distress, but that there might be equality (2 Cor. 8:13–14), so too we might suggest that a call for human self-limitation and generous consideration for others is not an unreasonable call to sacrifice human wellbeing in the interests of the flourishing of other species, but a call for a more equitable and considerate mode of relationship.

Yet all of this still remains rather vague and general. And indeed we must accept, I think, that there is no straightforward reading off of the right solution to ethical dilemmas from the pages of the Bible. This is the case with any moral issue, and all the more so in matters concerning ecology, where we are so dependent on modern scientific understanding to inform us about problems and their possible solutions. The Bible does not, and cannot, tell us what we should do in specific situations where we face some dilemma or problem, like how to halt the destruction of the Amazonian rainforest, or protect a threatened species of bird, or enable a system of agriculture to lessen its dependence on oil and oil-derived products. Moreover, even attempting to bring general orientating principles to bear on ethics quickly highlights how complex and uncertain is the task. So, for example, it is all very well to affirm the intrinsic goodness of all creation, but does this goodness include the malaria parasite or HIV? Some will quickly respond that such things are signs of the fallenness of creation, and that freeing the world from them is an act in keeping with the vision of creation's liberation from suffering and decay. But if the world as we know it emerged through the processes of evolution, as science currently understands them, then it is impossible to conceive of any time when creatures lived without the threats of parasites and viruses, or without the suffering and threat of predation; indeed, these very threats are intrinsic to the processes by which diversity and beauty emerged (see Southgate 2008b). Moreover, the elimination of even apparently harmful life-forms often has some knock-on effect on other species, affecting the balance of ecosystems. Perhaps the sense of working towards an eschatological vision of reconciliation and liberation helps here, but it clearly provides no easy solutions.

What then would the vision of peace and reconciliation suggest in terms of appropriate ethical outworkings? We have already noted some of the difficulties and disagreements in this regard (see ch. 8): it makes no sense to try to make wolves lie down with lambs, or insist that lions eat straw, since their very being and form is bound up with their activities and diet. One argument we have already mentioned is that for Christian vegetarianism: one possible and achievable action, inspired by the vision of peace among people and animals, is for humans to cease killing animals for food (see ch. 8). There are, nonetheless, questions to be raised about whether this is necessarily the best response, given the dependence of some animal species on human husbandry, the need for animals to be included in sustainable patterns of agriculture, and so on (see Southgate 2008a and Pollan 2006: 304–33 for illuminating discussions). But what this argument powerfully brings to light is the extent to which the guiding ethical vision would certainly seem to require a compassionate, generous, and careful treatment of animals, which affirms and respects their intrinsic worth. Another possibility, proposed by Christopher Southgate, is that humans should work to end the extinction of species. For Southgate, this would be an appropriate response to the vision of the liberation of creation, in which the children of God take the responsibility associated with their freedom and glory in Christ (see Southgate 2008b: 124–32). The loss of species is, of course, as Southgate notes, intrinsic to the evolutionary process; but his proposal is based on the conviction that we stand at a particular point in the eschatological story of salvation, at which certain actions which anticipate and reflect the future freedom of creation are appropriate. Another idea Southgate develops is that, in view of the impact of rapid (human-caused) climate change on non-human species, humans might practise the kind of "other-regard" I outlined above and act to relocate animals to new habitats, in a bid to try to ensure their survival and future flourishing (Southgate 2009).

However inspiring the vision of universal reconciliation, it is clear enough that reconciliation cannot mean an end to predation, nor indeed to competition (for scarce resources, living space, etc.), which is again intrinsic to the processes by which creatures co-exist and struggle to survive. What Southgate's ethical proposals might perhaps imply is a more scientifically cogent – but still ethically challenging – notion of reconciliation, one which seeks to create and maintain a kind of balanced and sustainable mutual co-existence, a peaceable creation in the sense that there is "space" for all to exist and to flourish, in which predation and killing is non-oppressive. It may sound nonsensical to talk of non-oppressive predation, but what I intend to signal is the difference between a situation where a population is hunted to the brink of extermination, and a situation where levels of predation allow healthy groups nonetheless to survive and flourish. This, of course, immediately raises questions about the extent to which humans should interfere, should seek to manage or influence the animal populations and ecosystems of our world, questions which take us right back to the issue of anthropocentrism. What Southgate's interesting proposals imply is that there is a need for humans to act, to take responsibility, and not simply to attempt to leave nature alone. This is a positive anthropocentrism, in the sense that it sees the human calling as implying a special responsibility, which must be borne and not shirked, for the wellbeing of our world. It is also a calling which, in its imitation of Christ, implies and requires a costly self-giving, what Southgate calls an "ethical kenosis", on the part of the powerful human species. Given the massive impact of human activity upon the planet, and the extent to which landscapes and species are, in many cases, already the product of interaction between humans and their environment, this call to responsibility would seem a more realistic appeal than one which calls for humans to leave nature alone.

An ecological biblical theology and ethics cannot, then, resolve the questions about how exactly it is right to act in response to specific situations and dilemmas. For such answers, we need all the information that contemporary science gives us. But I hope to have shown that the biblical tradition, critically and constructively engaged, can provide resources to reshape Christian theology and ethics, providing a renewed vision of the goodness, value, interconnectedness, beauty, calling, and peaceful reconciliation of all things, relativizing and challenging a long-entrenched focus on human welfare and human salvation, and reaching instead for a theology which fully embraces all created things, and provides a vision which shapes and guides human action in fostering the peaceable wellbeing of the whole world. We began this book with the classic argument of Lynn White Jr, who blamed the Christian worldview, shaped by the biblical creation stories, for creating our current ecological problems. Rather than reject religion, White saw religion as crucially important in shaping our worldviews, and thus our patterns of behaviour. He made, we recall, this striking claim: "More science and more technology are not going to get us out of the present ecological crisis until we find a new religion, or rethink our old one" (White 1967: 1206). What I hope to have shown in this book is that a critical and constructive engagement with the Bible, undertaken in a hermeutically-informed and ecologically-focused way, can indeed offer ways to "rethink" an old religion, in ways that resource a positive engagement with the ecological challenges that confront us.

Further reading

Conradie, Ernst M., "What on Earth is an Ecological Hermeneutics? Some Broad Parameters", in David G. Horrell, Cherryl Hunt, Christopher Southgate and Francesca Stavrakopoulou (eds), *Ecological Hermeneutics: Biblical, Historical, and Theological Perspectives* (London and New York: T. & T. Clark, forthcoming).

———, "The Road Towards an Ecological Biblical and Theological Hermeneutics", *Scriptura* 93 (2006) 305–14.

Barton, Stephen C., "New Testament Eschatology and the Ecological Crisis in Theological and Ecclesial Perspective", in David G. Horrell, Cherryl Hunt, Christopher Southgate and Francesca Stavrakopoulou (eds), *Ecological Hermeneutics: Biblical, Historical, and Theological Perspectives* (London and New York: T. & T. Clark, forthcoming).

Finger, Thomas, *Evangelicals, Eschatology, and the Environment* (The Scholars Circle; Wynnewood, PA: Evangelical Environmental Network, 1998).

Horrell, David G., Hunt, Cherryl and Southgate, Christopher, *The Green Paul: Rereading the Apostle in an Age of Ecological Crisis* (Waco, TX: Baylor University Press, forthcoming).

Southgate, Christopher, "Protological and Eschatological Vegetarianism", in Rachel Muers and David Grumett (eds), *Eating and Believing: Interdisciplinary Perspectives on Vegetarianism and Theology* (London and New York: T. & T. Clark, 2008), 247–65.

———, *The Groaning of Creation: God, Evolution, and the Problem of Evil* (Louisville, KY: Westminster John Knox, 2008).

———, "The New Days of Noah?: Assisted Migration as an Ethical Imperative in an Era of Climate Change", in Celia Deane-Drummond and David Clough (eds), *Creaturely Theology* (London: SCM, 2009), 249–65.

Clough, David, *On Animals: Theology* (London and New York: T. & T. Clark, forthcoming).

BIBLIOGRAPHY

Adams, Edward (2007), *The Stars Will Fall From Heaven: Cosmic Catastrophe in the New Testament and its World* (Library of New Testament Studies 347; London and New York: T. & T. Clark).

Allen, Leslie C. (1983), *Psalms 101–150* (WBC 21; Waco, TX: Word).

Anderson, Bernhard W. (1984), "Creation and Ecology", in Bernhard W. Anderson, *Creation in the Old Testament* (Philadelphia, PA/London: Fortress/ SPCK), 152–71.

Balabanski, Vicky (2008), "Critiquing Anthropocentric Cosmology: Retrieving a Stoic 'Permeation Cosmology' in Colossians 1:15–20", in Norman C. Habel and Peter Trudinger (eds), *Exploring Ecological Hermeneutics* (SBL Symposium Series 46; Atlanta, GA: Society of Biblical Literature), 151–59.

—— (forthcoming), "Hellenistic Cosmology and the Letter to the Colossians: Towards an Ecological Hermeneutic", in David G. Horrell, Cherryl Hunt, Christopher Southgate, and Francesca Stavrakopoulou (eds), *Ecological Hermeneutics: Biblical, Historical, and Theological Perspectives* (London and New York: T. & T. Clark).

Baranzke, Heike and Lamberty-Zielinski, Hedwig (1995), "Lynn White und das Dominium Terrae (Gen 1,28b). Ein Beitrag zu einer doppelten Wirkungsgeschichte", *Biblische Notizen* 76: 32—61.

Barclay, John M. G. (1997), *Colossians and Philemon* (NTG; Sheffield: Sheffield Academic Press).

Barr, James (1972), "Man and Nature – The Ecological Controversy and the Old Testament", *Bulletin of the John Rylands Library* 55: 9–32.

Barth, Karl (1957), *Church Dogmatics II.1: The Doctrine of God* (Edinburgh: T. & T. Clark).

Barton, John (2001), *Joel and Obadiah: A Commentary* (OTL; Louisville, KY: Westminster John Knox).

Barton, Stephen C. (forthcoming), "New Testament Eschatology and the Ecological Crisis in Theological and Ecclesial Perspective", in David G. Horrell, Cherryl Hunt, Christopher Southgate, and Francesca Stavrakopoulou (eds), *Ecological Hermeneutics: Biblical, Historical, and Theological Perspectives* (London and New York: T. & T. Clark).

Bauckham, Richard J. (1983), *Jude, 2 Peter* (WBC 50; Waco, TX: Word).

—— (1994), "Jesus and the Wild Animals (Mark 1:13): A Christological Image for an Ecological Age", in Joel B. Green and Max Turner (eds), *Jesus of Nazareth:*

Lord and Christ. Essays on the Historical Jesus and New Testament Christology (Grand Rapids, MI/Carlisle: Eerdmans/Paternoster), 3–21.

—— (2000), "Stewardship and Relationship", in R. J. Berry (ed.), *The Care of Creation* (Leicester: IVP), 99–106.

—— (2002a), *God and the Crisis of Freedom: Biblical and Contemporary Perspectives* (Louisville, KY/London: Westminster John Knox).

—— (2002b), "Joining Creation's Praise of God", *Ecotheology* 7: 45–59.

Beisner, E. Calvin (1997), *Where Garden Meets Wilderness: Evangelical Entry into the Environmental Debate* (Grand Rapids, MI: Acton Institute for the Study of Religion and Liberty/Eerdmans).

Berry, R. J. (ed.), (2000), *The Care of Creation* (Leicester: IVP).

Blenkinsopp, Joseph (2004), *Treasures Old and New: Essays in the Theology of the Pentateuch* (Grand Rapids, MI: Eerdmans).

Boff, Leonardo, and Clodovis Boff (1987), *Introducing Liberation Theology* (Maryknoll, NY/Tunbridge Wells: Orbis/Burns & Oates).

Boring, M. Eugene (1989), *Revelation* (Interpretation; Louisville, KY: Westminster John Knox).

Bouma-Prediger, Steven (2001), *For the Beauty of the Earth: A Christian Vision for Creation Care* (Grand Rapids, MI: Baker Academic).

Boyer, Paul (1992), *When Time Shall Be No More: Prophecy Belief in Modern American Culture* (Cambridge, MA/London: Belknap/Harvard University Press).

Braaten, Laurie J. (2006), "Earth Community in Joel 1–2: A Call to Identify with the Rest of Creation", *Horizons in Biblical Theology* 28: 113–29.

—— (2008), "Earth Community in Joel: A Call to Identify with the Rest of Creation", in Norman C. Habel and Peter Trudinger (eds), *Exploring Ecological Hermeneutics* (SBL Symposium Series 46; Atlanta, GA: Society of Biblical Literature), 63–74.

Brett, Mark G. (2000), "Earthing the Human in Genesis 1–3", in Norman C. Habel and Shirley Wurst (eds), *The Earth Story in Genesis* (EB 2; Sheffield: Sheffield Academic Press), 73–86.

Brooke, George J. (2001), "Additions to Daniel: the Prayer of Azariah, the Song of the Three Jews, Susanna, Bel and the Dragon", in John Barton and John Muddiman (eds), *The Oxford Bible Commentary* (Oxford: OUP), 704–11.

Bruggemann, Walter (1982), *Genesis* (Interpretation; Atlanta, GA: John Knox).

Byrne, Brendan (2000), "Creation Groaning: An Earth Bible Reading of Romans 8.18-22", in Norman C. Habel (ed.), *Readings from the Perspective of Earth* (EB 1; Sheffield: Sheffield Academic Press), 193–203.

—— (forthcoming), "An Ecological Reading of Rom. 8:19–22: Possibilities and Hesitations", in David G. Horrell, Cherryl Hunt, Christopher Southgate, and Francesca Stavrakopoulou (eds), *Ecological Hermeneutics: Biblical, Historical, and Theological Perspectives* (London and New York: T. & T. Clark).

Caird, George B. (1966), *The Revelation of St John the Divine* (BNTC; London: A. & C. Black).

Calvin, John (1965 [1554]) *Genesis* (Edinburgh: Banner of Truth Trust).

Carley, Keith (2000), "Psalm 8: An Apology for Domination", in Norman C. Habel (ed.), *Readings from the Perspective of Earth* (EB 1; Sheffield: Sheffield Academic Press), 111–24.

Carson, Rachel (2000 [1962]), *Silent Spring* (Penguin Classics edn.; London and New York: Penguin).

Chester, Andrew N. and Martin, Ralph P. (1994), *The Theology of the Letters of James, Peter and Jude* (New Testament Theology; Cambridge: Cambridge University Press).

Childs, Brevard S. (2001), *Isaiah* (OTL; Louisville, KY: Westminster John Knox).

Clifford, Paula (2007), *"All Creation Groaning": A Theological Approach to Climate Change and Development*, (London: Christian Aid).

Clough, David (forthcoming), *On Animals: Theology* (London and New York: T. & T. Clark).

Coad, Dominic (2009), "Creation's Praise of God: A Proposal for a Theology of the Non-Human Creation", *Theology* 112: 181–89.

Coggins, Richard J. (2000) *Joel and Amos* (New Century Bible Commentary; Sheffield: Sheffield Academic Press).

Collins, John J. (1983) "Sibylline Oracles", in James H. Charlesworth (ed.), *Old Testament Pseudepigrapha* (Vol 1; New York: Doubleday), 317–472.

Conradie, Ernst M. (2004), "Towards an Ecological Biblical Hermeneutics: A Review Essay on the Earth Bible Project", *Scriptura* 85: 123–35.

—— (2006), "The Road Towards an Ecological Biblical and Theological Hermeneutics", *Scriptura* 93: 305–14.

—— (2008), *Angling for Interpretation: A First Guide to Biblical, Theological and Contextual Hermeneutics* (Study Guides in Religion and Theology 13; Stellenbosch: SUN Press).

—— (2009), "Interpreting the Bible amidst Ecological Degradation", *Theology* 112: 199–207.

—— (forthcoming), "What on Earth is an Ecological Hermeneutics? Some Broad Parameters", in David G. Horrell, Cherryl Hunt, Christopher Southgate, and Francesca Stavrakopoulou (eds), *Ecological Hermeneutics: Biblical, Historical, and Theological Perspectives* (London and New York: T. & T. Clark).

Cooper, Tim (1990), *Green Christianity: Caring for the Whole Creation* (London: Spire/ Hodder & Stoughton).

Craigie, Peter C. (1983), *Psalms 1–50* (WBC 19; Waco, TX: Word).

Crenshaw, James L. (1992), "When Form and Content Collide: The Theology of Job 38:1–40:5", in Richard J. Clifford and John J. Collins (eds), *Creation in the Biblical Traditions* (Catholic Biblical Quarterly Monograph Series 24; Washington, DC: Catholic Biblical Association), 70–84.

Cumbey, Constance E. (1983), *The Hidden Dangers of the Rainbow: The New Age Movement and Our Coming Age of Barbarism* (Shreveport: Huntington House).

Day, John (1990), *Psalms* (OTG; Sheffield: Sheffield Academic Press).

Deane-Drummond, Celia E. (2000), *Creation through Wisdom: Theology and the New Biology* (Edinburgh: T. & T. Clark).

Deane-Drummond, Celia E. (2004), *The Ethics of Nature* (New Dimensions to Religious Ethics 4; Oxford and Malden, MA: Blackwell).

Dell, Katharine (1994), "'Green' Ideas in the Wisdom Tradition", *Scottish Journal of Theology* 47: 423–51.

Dunn, James D. G. (1988), *Romans 1–8* (WBC 38A; Dallas, TX: Word Books).

—— (1996), *The Epistles to the Colossians and to Philemon* (New International Greek Testament Commentary; Grand Rapids, MI/Carlisle: Eerdmans/ Paternoster).

Dyer, Keith D. (2002), "When Is the End Not the End? The Fate of Earth in Biblical Eschatology (Mark 13)", in Norman C. Habel and Vicky Balabanski (eds), *The Earth Story in the New Testament* (EB 5; Sheffield: Sheffield Academic Press), 44–56.

Dyrness, William (1987), "Stewardship of the Earth in the Old Testament", in Wesley Granberg-Michaelson (ed.), *Tending the Garden* (Grand Rapids, MI: Eerdmans), 50–65.

Earth Bible Team, The (2000), "Guiding Ecojustice Principles", in Norman C. Habel (ed.), *Readings from the Perspective of Earth* (EB 1; Sheffield: Sheffield Academic Press), 38–53.

—— (2002), "Ecojustice Hermeneutics: Reflections and Challenges", in Norman C. Habel and Vicky Balabanski (eds), *The Earth Story in the New Testament* (EB 5; Sheffield: Sheffield Academic Press), 1–14.

Eckberg, Douglas Lee and Blocker, T. Jean (1996), "Christianity, Environmentalism, and the Theoretical Problem of Fundamentalism", *Journal for the Scientific Study of Religion* 35: 343–355.

Epp, Eldon J. (2005), *Junia: The First Woman Apostle* (Minneapolis, MN: Fortress).

Evangelical Climate Initiative (2006), http://christiansandclimate.org/learn/call-to-action/ [accessed 15 Sept 2008].

Finger, Thomas (1998), *Evangelicals, Eschatology, and the Environment* (The Scholars Circle; Wynnewood, PA: Evangelical Environmental Network).

Fretheim, Terence E. (1987), "Nature's Praise of God in the Psalms", *Ex Auditu* 3: 16–30.

—— (2005), *God and World in the Old Testament: A Relational Theology of Creation* (Nashville, TN: Abingdon).

Furnish, Victor Paul (1968), *Theology and Ethics in Paul* (Nashville, TN: Abingdon).

Gordley, Matthew E. (2007), *The Colossian Hymn in Context: An Exegesis in Light of Jewish and Greco-Roman Hymnic and Epistolary Conventions* (WUNT 2.228; Tübingen: Mohr Siebeck).

Granberg-Michaelson, Wesley (1987a), "Introduction: Identification or Mastery?" in Wesley Granberg-Michaelson (ed.), *Tending the Garden* (Grand Rapids, MI: Eerdmans), 1–5.

—— (ed.), (1987b), *Tending the Garden* (Grand Rapids, MI: Eerdmans).

Gribben, Crawford (2004), "Rapture Fictions and the Changing Evangelical Condition", *Literature and Theology* 18: 77–94.

Grove, Jim (2008), "Hellfire is the real global warming", http://ydr.inyork.com/ci_11103726 [accessed 15 Dec 2008].

Grudem, Wayne (1994), *Systematic Theology: An Introduction to Biblical Doctrine* (Leicester: IVP).

Gutiérrez, Gustavo (1974 [1971]), *A Theology of Liberation* (London: SCM).

Habel, Norman C. (2000a), "Introducing the Earth Bible", in Norman C. Habel (ed.), *Readings from the Perspective of Earth* (EB 1; Sheffield: Sheffield Academic Press), 25–37.

——— (2000b), "Geophany: The Earth Story in Genesis 1", in Norman C. Habel and Shirley Wurst (eds), *The Earth Story in Genesis* (EB 2; Sheffield: Sheffield Academic Press), 34–48.

——— (2001a), "'Is the Wild Ox Willing to Serve You?' Challenging the Mandate to Dominate", in Norman C. Habel and Shirley Wurst (eds), *The Earth Story in Wisdom Traditions* (EB 3; Sheffield: Sheffield Academic Press), 179–89.

——— (ed.), (2000c), *Readings from the Perspective of Earth* (EB 1; Sheffield: Sheffield Academic Press).

——— (ed.), (2001b), *The Earth Story in the Psalms and the Prophets* (EB 4; Sheffield: Sheffield Academic Press).

Habel, Norman C. and Wurst, Shirley (eds) (2000), *The Earth Story in Genesis* (EB 2; Sheffield: Sheffield Academic Press).

——— (eds) (2001), *The Earth Story in Wisdom Traditions* (EB 3; Sheffield: Sheffield Academic Press).

Habel, Norman C. and Balabanski, Vicky (eds) (2002), *The Earth Story in the New Testament* (EB 5; Sheffield: Sheffield Academic Press).

Hall, Douglas John (1990 [1982]), *The Steward: A Biblical Symbol Come of Age* (Revised edn.; Garden Rapids, MI/New York: Eerdmans/Friendship Press).

Harrison, Peter (1999), "Subduing the Earth: Genesis 1, Early Modern Science, and the Exploitation of Nature", *Journal of Religion* 79: 86–109.

Hartley, John E. (2000), *Genesis* (New International Biblical Commentary 1; Peabody, MA: Hendrickson).

Hayes, Katherine M. (2002), *"The Earth Mourns": Prophetic Metaphor and Oral Aesthetic* (SBL Academia Biblica 8; Atlanta, GA: Society of Biblical Literature).

Hays, Richard B. (1997), *The Moral Vision of the New Testament* (Edinburgh: T. & T. Clark).

Hiebert, Theodore (2008), "Air, the First Sacred Thing: The Conception of רוח in the Hebrew Scriptures", in Norman C. Habel and Peter Trudinger (eds), *Exploring Ecological Hermeneutics* (SBL Symposium Series 46; Atlanta, GA: Society of Biblical Literature), 9–19.

Hill, Brennan R. (1998), *Christian Faith and the Environment: Making Vital Connections* (Maryknoll: Orbis).

Hooker, Morna D. (1991), *The Gospel According to Saint Mark* (BNTC; London: A. & C. Black).

Horrell, David G. (2005), *Solidarity and Difference: A Contemporary Reading of Paul's Ethics* (London and New York: T. & T. Clark).

——— (2006), *An Introduction to the Study of Paul* (2nd edn; London and New York: T. & T. Clark).

——— (2008), "Biblical Vegetarianism? A Critical and Constructive Assessment", in Rachel Muers and David Grumett (eds), *Eating and Believing:*

Interdisciplinary Perspectives on Vegetarianism and Theology (London and New York: T. & T. Clark), 44–59.

—— (forthcoming a), "Ecojustice in the Bible? Pauline Contributions to an Ecological Theology", in Matthew J. M. Coomber (ed.), *Bible and Justice: Ancient Texts, Modern Challenges* (London and Oakville, CT: Equinox).

—— (forthcoming b), "*The Green Bible*: A Timely Idea Deeply Flawed", *Expository Times* 121 (January 2010 in press).

Horrell, David G. and Coad, Dominic (forthcoming), "'The Stones Would Cry Out' (Luke 19:40): A Lukan Contribution to a Hermeneutics of Creation's Praise", *Scottish Journal of Theology*.

Horrell, David G., Hunt, Cherryl and Southgate, Christopher (2008) "Appeals to the Bible in Ecotheology and Environmental Ethics: A Typology of Hermeneutical Stances", *Studies in Christian Ethics* 21: 219–38.

Horrell, David G., Hunt, Cherryl and Southgate, Christopher (forthcoming), *The Green Paul: Rereading the Apostle in an Age of Ecological Crisis* (Waco, TX: Baylor University Press).

Hubbard, Moyer V. (2002), *New Creation in Paul's Letters and Thought* (Society for New Testament Studies Monograph Series 119; Cambridge: CUP).

Hunt, Cherryl, Horrell, David G. and Southgate, Christopher (2008), "An Environmental Mantra? Ecological Interest in Romans 8:19–23 and a Modest Proposal for its Narrative Interpretation", *Journal of Theological Studies* 59: 546–79.

Hunt, Cherryl (2009), "Beyond Anthropocentrism: Towards a Re-reading of Pauline Ethics", *Theology* 112: 190–98.

Hunt, Dave (1983), *Peace Prosperity and the Coming Holocaust: The New Age Movement in Prophecy* (Eugene, OR: Harvest House).

Hunter, Alastair (2006), *Wisdom Literature* (London: SCM).

IPCC (2007) *Climate Change 2007: Synthesis Report*, at http://www.ipcc.ch/publications_and_data/publications_ipcc_fourth_assessment_report_synthesis_report.htm [accessed 20 October 2009].

Jewett, Robert (2004), "The Corruption and Redemption of Creation: Reading Rom 8:18–23 within the Imperial Context", in Richard A. Horsley (ed.), *Paul and the Roman Imperial Order* (Harrisburg, PA: Trinity Press International), 25–46.

Johnston, Robert K. (1987), "Wisdom Literature and Its Contribution to a Biblical Environmental Ethic", in Wesley Granberg-Michaelson (ed.), *Tending the Garden* (Grand Rapids, MI: Eerdmans), 66–82.

Jones, James (2003), *Jesus and the Earth* (London: SPCK).

Kaiser, Otto (1983), *Isaiah 1–12: A Commentary* (2nd edn, OTL; London: SCM).

Klassen, William (1984), "Musonius Rufus, Jesus, and Paul: Three First-Century Feminists", in John C. Hurd and Peter Richardson (eds), *From Jesus to Paul: Studies in Honour of Francis Wright Beare* (Ontario: Wilfrid Laurier University Press), 185–206.

Kovacs, Judith, and Rowland, Christopher (2004), *Revelation* (Blackwell Bible Commentaries; Oxford and Malden, MA: Blackwell).

Kraus, Hans-Joachim (1989), *Psalms 60–150: A Commentary* (Minneapolis, MN: Augsburg).

Lear, Linda (1999), "Afterword", in Rachel Carson, *Silent Spring* (Penguin Classics edn.; London and New York: Penguin), 258–64.

Leske, Adrian M. (2002), "Matthew 6:25–34: Human Anxiety and the Natural World", in Norman C. Habel and Vicky Balabanski (eds), *The Earth Story in the New Testament* (EB 5; Sheffield: Sheffield Academic Press), 15–27.

Limburg, James (2000), *Psalms* (Westminster Bible Companion; Louisville, KY: Westminster John Knox).

Linzey, Andrew (1994), *Animal Theology* (London: SPCK).

Lohfink, Norbert (1994), *Theology of the Pentateuch: Themes of the Priestly Narrative and Deuteronomy* (Edinburgh: T. & T. Clark).

Lucas, Ernest (1999), "The New Testament Teaching on the Environment", *Transformation*, 16:3: 93–99 (reprinted in Sam Berry *et al.*, *A Christian Approach to the Environment*, The John Ray Initiative, 2005).

Maier, Harry O. (2002), "There's a New World Coming! Reading the Apocalypse in the Shadow of the Canadian Rockies", in Norman C. Habel and Vicky Balabanski (eds), *The Earth Story in the New Testament* (EB 5; London and New York: Sheffield Academic Press), 166–79.

—— (forthcoming), "Green Millennialism: American Evangelicals, Environmentalism, and the Book of Revelation", in David G. Horrell, Cherryl Hunt, Christopher Southgate, and Francesca Stavrakopoulou (eds), *Ecological Hermeneutics: Biblical, Historical, and Theological Perspectives* (London and New York: T. & T. Clark).

Martin-Schramm, James B. and Stivers, Robert L. (2003), *Christian Environmental Ethics: A Case Study Approach* (Maryknoll, NY: Orbis).

Maslin, Mark (2007 [2002]), *Global Warming* (Revised edn., WorldLife Library; Grantown-on-Spey, Scotland: Colin Baxter Photography).

Mason, Rex (1994), *Zephaniah, Habakkuk, Joel* (OTG; Sheffield: Sheffield Academic Press).

McDonagh, Sean (1990), *The Greening of the Church* (Maryknoll, NY: Orbis).

—— (1994), *Passion for the Earth* (London: Geoffrey Chapman).

McKibben, Bill (1994), *The Comforting Whirlwind: God, Job, and the Scale of Creation* (Grand Rapids, MI: Eerdmans).

Meeks, Wayne A. (1996), "The 'Haustafeln' and American Slavery: A Hermeneutical Challenge", in Eugene H. Lovering Jr and Jerry L. Sumney (eds), *Theology and Ethics in Paul and His Interpreters: Essays in Honor of Victor Paul Furnish* (Nashville, TN: Abingdon), 232–53.

Mell, Ulrich (1989), *Neue Schöpfung: Eine traditionsgeschichtliche und exegetische Studie zu einem soteriologischen Grundsatz paulinischer Theologie* (Beihefte zur Zeitschrift für die neutestamentliche Wissenschaft 56; Berlin/New York: De Gruyter).

Moo, Douglas J. (2006), "Nature in the New Creation: New Testament Eschatology and the Environment", *Journal of the Evangelical Theological Society* 49: 449–88.

Morgan, Jonathan (2009), "Transgressing, Puking, Covenanting: The Character of Land in Leviticus", *Theology* 112: 172–80.

Myers, Ched (1988), *Binding the Strong Man: A Political Reading of Mark's Story of Jesus* (Maryknoll, NY: Orbis).

Northcott, Michael S. (1996), *The Environment and Christian Ethics* (New Studies in Christian Ethics; Cambridge: CUP).

Ntreh, Abotchie (2001), "The Survival of Earth: An African Reading of Psalm 104", in Norman C. Habel (ed.), *The Earth Story in the Psalms and the Prophets* (EB 4; Sheffield: Sheffield Academic Press), 98–108.

Olley, John W. (2000), "Mixed Blessings for Animals: The Contrasts of Genesis 9", in Norman C. Habel and Shirley Wurst (eds), *The Earth Story in Genesis* (EB 2; Sheffield: Sheffield Academic Press), 131–39.

—— (2001), "'The Wolf, the Lamb, and a Little Child': Transforming the Diverse Earth Community in Isaiah", in Norman C. Habel (ed.), *The Earth Story in the Psalms and the Prophets* (EB 4; Sheffield: Sheffield Academic Press), 219–29.

Orr, David W. (2005), "Armageddon Versus Extinction", *Conservation Biology* 19: 290–92.

Osborn, Lawrence (1993), *Guardians of Creation: Nature in Theology and the Christian Life* (Leicester: Apollos).

Palmer, Clare (1992), "Stewardship: A Case Study in Environmental Ethics", in Ian Ball, *et al.*, *The Earth Beneath: A Critical Guide to Green Theology* (London: SPCK), 67–86 (Reprinted in R. J. Berry [ed.] *Environmental Stewardship: Critical Perspectives, Past and Present* [London and New York: T. & T. Clark, 2006]).

Patrick, Dale (2001), "Divine Creative Power and the Decentering of Creation: The Subtext of the Lord's Addresses to Job", in Norman C. Habel and Shirley Wurst (eds), *The Earth Story in Wisdom Traditions* (EB 3; Sheffield: Sheffield Academic Press), 103–15.

Pollan, Michael (2006), *The Omnivore's Dilemma* (London: Bloomsbury).

Rad, Gerhard von (1963), *Genesis: A Commentary* (2nd edn, OTL; London: SCM).

Reid, Duncan (2000), "Setting Aside the Ladder to Heaven: Revelation 21: 1–22:5 from the Perspective of the Earth", in Norman C. Habel (ed.), *Readings from the Perspective of Earth* (EB 1; Sheffield: Sheffield Academic Press), 232–45.

Reumann, John (1992), *Stewardship and the Economy of God* (Grand Rapids, MI and Indianapolis, IN: Eerdmans/The Ecumenical Center for Stewardship Studies).

Rogerson, John W. (1991), *Genesis 1–11* (OTG; Sheffield: Sheffield Academic Press).

—— (2007), *According to the Scriptures? The Challenge of Using the Bible in Social, Moral and Political Questions* (Biblical Challenges in the Contemporary World; London and Oakville, CT: Equinox).

Rowland, C. C. (1990), "Apocalyptic", in Richard J. Coggins and J. Leslie Houlden (eds), *A Dictionary of Biblical Interpretation* (London: SCM), 34–36.

Russell, David M. (1996), *The "New Heavens and New Earth": Hope for the Creation in Jewish Apocalyptic and the New Testament* (Studies in Biblical Apocalyptic Literature; Philadelphia, PA: Visionary Press).

Sanders, E. P. (1985), *Jesus and Judaism* (London: SCM).

Santmire, H. Paul (2000), *Nature Reborn. The Ecological and Cosmic Promise of Christian Theology* (Minneapolis, MN: Fortress Press).

Schweitzer, Albert (2000 [1913]), *The Quest of the Historical Jesus* (London: SCM).

Sherkat, Darren E. and Ellison, Christopher G. (2007), "Structuring the Religion-Environment Connection: Identifying Religious Influences on Environmental Concern and Activism", *Journal for the Scientific Study of Religion* 46: 71–85.

Sittler, Joseph (2000a [1954]), "A Theology for Earth", in Steven Bouma-Prediger and Peter Bakken (eds), *Evocations of Grace: The Writings of Joseph Sittler on Ecology, Theology and Ethics* (Grand Rapids, MI: Eerdmans), 20–31.

—— (2000b [1962]), "Called to Unity", in Steven Bouma-Prediger and Peter Bakken (eds), *Evocations of Grace: The Writings of Joseph Sittler on Ecology, Theology and Ethics* (Grand Rapids, MI: Eerdmans), 38–50.

Southgate, Christopher (2006), "Stewardship and its Competitors: a Spectrum of Relationships between Humans and the Non-human Creation", in R. J. Berry (ed.), *Environmental Stewardship: Critical Perspectives, Past and Present* (London and New York: T. & T. Clark), 185–95.

—— (2008a), "Protological and Eschatological Vegetarianism", in Rachel Muers and David Grumett (eds), *Eating and Believing: Interdisciplinary Perspectives on Vegetarianism and Theology* (London and New York: T. & T. Clark), 247–65.

—— (2008b), *The Groaning of Creation: God, Evolution, and the Problem of Evil* (Louisville, KY: Westminster John Knox).

—— (2009), "The New Days of Noah?: Assisted Migration as an Ethical Imperative in an Era of Climate Change", in Celia Deane-Drummond and David Clough (eds), *Creaturely Theology* (London: SCM), 249–65.

Stettler, Christian (2000), *Der Kolosserhymnus: Untersuchungen zu Form, traditionsgeschichtlichem Hintergrund und Aussage von Kol 1, 15–20* (WUNT 2.131; Tübingen: Mohr Siebeck).

Still, Todd D. (2004), "Eschatology in Colossians: How Realized is it?" *New Testament Studies* 50: 125–38.

Strandberg, Todd (no date), "Bible Prophecy and Environmentalism", at http://www.raptureready.com/rr-environmental.html [accessed 18 December 2008].

Strickland, Spencer (2008), "Beware of Global Warming! (2 Peter 3:6–7)", http://jeremiahdanielmccarver.wordpress.com/2008/08/07/beware-of-global-warming-2-peter-36-7/ [accessed 15 December 2008].

Swartley, Willard M. (1983), *Slavery, Sabbath, War and Women: Case Issues in Biblical Interpretation* (Scottdale, PA and Waterloo, Ont.: Herald).

Sweet, John (1979), *Revelation* (New Testament Commentaries; London: SCM).

Theissen, Gerd (1993), *Social Reality and the Early Christians: Theology, Ethics, and the World of the New Testament* (Edinburgh: T. & T. Clark).

Theissen, Gerd and Merz, Annette (1998), *The Historical Jesus: A Comprehensive Guide* (London: SCM).

Thielicke, Helmut (1966), *Theological Ethics. Volume 1: Foundations* (Grand Rapids, MI: Eerdmans).

Towner, W. Sibley (1996), "The Future of Nature", *Interpretation* 50: 27–35.

Trible, Phyllis (1978), *God and the Rhetoric of Sexuality* (London: SCM).

—— (1993), "Treasures Old and New: Biblical Theology and the Challenge of Feminism", in Francis Watson (ed.), *The Open Text: New Directions for Biblical Studies?* (London: SCM), 32–56.

Van Kooten, George H. (2003), *Cosmic Christology in Paul and the Pauline School* (WUNT 2.171; Tübingen: Mohr Siebeck).

Walker-Jones, Arthur (2001), "Psalm 104: A Celebration of the *Vanua*", in Norman C. Habel (ed.), *The Earth Story in the Psalms and the Prophets* (EB 4; Sheffield: Sheffield Academic Press), 84–97.

Wallace, Howard N. (2000), "Rest for the Earth? Another Look at Genesis 2: 1–3", in Norman C. Habel and Shirley Wurst (eds), *The Earth Story in Genesis* (EB 2; Sheffield: Sheffield Academic Press), 49–59.

Watson, Francis (2008), "Hermeneutics and the Doctrine of Scripture: Why They Need Each Other", paper presented at the Australasian Theological Forum in Canberra, (November 2008, publication forthcoming).

—— (forthcoming), "In the Beginning: Irenaeus, Creation, and the Environment", in David G. Horrell, Cherryl Hunt, Christopher Southgate, and Francesca Stavrakopoulou (eds), *Ecological Hermeneutics: Biblical, Historical, and Theological Perspectives* (London and New York: T. & T. Clark).

Webb, Stephen H. (2001), *Good Eating* (Grand Rapids, MI: Brazos).

Wenham, Gordon J. (1987), *Genesis 1–15* (WBC 1; Waco, TX: Word).

Westermann, Claus (1974a), *Creation* (London: SPCK).

—— (1974b), *Genesis* (Vol 1; Biblischer Kommentar, Altes Testament; Neukirchen-Vluyn: Neukirchener).

—— (1988), *Genesis*, trans. David E. Orton (Edinburgh: T. & T. Clark).

White, Lynn, Jr (1967), "The Historical Roots of our Ecologic Crisis", *Science* 155: 1203–207.

Wilkinson, Loren, (Ed.) (1980), *Earthkeeping: Christian Stewardship of Natural Resources* (Grand Rapids, MI: Eerdmans).

Wright, N. T. (1991), *The Climax of the Covenant: Christ and the Law in Pauline Theology* (Edinburgh: T. & T. Clark).

—— (1992), *The New Testament and the People of God* (London: SPCK).

—— (1996), *Jesus and the Victory of God* (London: SPCK).

—— (1999), *New Heavens, New Earth: the Biblical Picture of Christian Hope* (Cambridge: Grove).

Wurst, Shirley (2000), "'Beloved, Come Back to Me!' Ground's Theme Song in Genesis 3?" in Norman C. Habel and Shirley Wurst (eds), *The Earth Story in Genesis* (EB 2; Sheffield: Sheffield Academic Press), 87–104.

Yarbro Collins, Adela (2007), *Mark: A Commentary* (Hermeneia; Minneapolis, MN: Fortress).

Index of biblical texts

Breinigsville, PA USA
14 February 2011
255428BV00004B/10/P

3 4711 00208 7833

9 781845 536220